NEW DIRECTIONS FOR INSTITUTIONAL RESEARCH

J. Fredericks Volkwein, *Pennsylvania State University*
EDITOR-IN-CHIEF

Larry H. Litten, *Consortium on Financing Higher Education,*
Cambridge, Massachusetts
ASSOCIATE EDITOR

Information Technology in Higher Education: Assessing Its Impact and Planning for the Future

Richard N. Katz, Julia A. Rudy
EDUCAUSE

EDITORS

Number 102, Summer 1999

JOSSEY-BASS PUBLISHERS
San Francisco

INFORMATION TECHNOLOGY IN HIGHER EDUCATION: ASSESSING ITS IMPACT
AND PLANNING FOR THE FUTURE
Richard N. Katz, Julia A. Rudy (eds.)
New Directions for Institutional Research, no. 102
Volume XXVI, Number 2
J. Fredericks Volkwein, Editor-in-Chief

New Directions for Institutional Research is indexed in *College Student
Personnel Abstracts, Contents Pages in Education,* and *Current Index to Journals in Education* (ERIC).

Microfilm copies of issues and chapters are available in 16mm and 35mm,
as well as microfiche in 105mm, through University Microfilms Inc., 300
North Zeeb Road, Ann Arbor, Michigan 48106–1346.

ISSN 0271-0579   ISBN 0-7879-1409-6

NEW DIRECTIONS FOR INSTITUTIONAL RESEARCH is part of The Jossey-Bass
Higher and Adult Education Series and is published quarterly by Jossey-
Bass Inc., Publishers, 350 Sansome Street, San Francisco, California
94104-1342 (publication number USPS 098-830). Periodicals postage
paid at San Francisco, California, and at additional mailing offices. POST-
MASTER: Send address changes to New Directions for Institutional
Research, Jossey-Bass Inc., Publishers, 350 Sansome Street, San Francisco,
California 94104-1342.

SUBSCRIPTIONS cost $56.00 for individuals and $95.00 for institutions,
agencies, and libraries.

EDITORIAL CORRESPONDENCE should be sent to J. Fredericks Volkwein,
Center for the Study of Higher Education, Pennsylvania State University,
403 South Allen Street, Suite 104, University Park, PA 16801-5252.

Photograph of the library by Michael Graves at San Juan Capistrano by
Chad Slattery © 1984. All rights reserved.

www.josseybass.com

Printed in the United States of America on acid-free recycled paper containing 100 percent recovered waste paper, of which at least 20 percent is
postconsumer waste.

EDUCAUSE

EDUCAUSE is an international nonprofit association with offices in Boulder, Colorado, and Washington, D.C. The association is dedicated to helping shape and enable transformational change in higher education through the introduction, use, and management of information resources and technologies in teaching, learning, scholarship, research, and institutional management. EDUCAUSE activities include an educational program of conferences, workshops, seminars, and institutes; a variety of print and on-line publications; strategic/policy initiatives such as the National Learning Infrastructure Initiative (NLII) and the Net@EDU program; a research and development program; and extensive Web-based information services. Current membership includes nearly 1,700 campuses and more than 150 corporations. To find out more about EDUCAUSE membership—and for the most up-to-date information about EDUCAUSE programs, initiatives, and services—visit the EDUCAUSE World Wide Web site at www.educause.edu or send e-mail to info@educause.edu.

SCT Education Systems, a major software and services company, serves more than 1,280 colleges and universities in the United States and in 26 countries worldwide. SCT has provided information systems to colleges and universities for more than thirty years, pioneering on-line, integrated administrative solutions for higher education. Today SCT continues to lead the way with the first Web-enabled student information product on the market with viewing and updating capabilities. SCT helped introduce the concept of outsourcing, or computer services partnerships with education institutions, providing on-site management, planning, and staffing of data processing operations. SCT offers a distance and on-line learning solution that provides total support for course content and delivery at a distance. The company recently introduced an event-driven, personalized Web user interface linking an institution's administrative and curricular components for delivery of e-mail, collaboration tools, customized personal and campus content, and e-commerce from within a secure environment. For more information about SCT, visit www.sctcorp.com.

ACKNOWLEDGMENTS

WE HAVE HAD the pleasure of reading volumes from the *New Directions for Institutional Research* series for more than a decade. It was therefore an exceptional honor and pleasure to be invited to serve as editors for this volume. Higher education is a complex and ever evolving enterprise and the *NDIR* volumes have long helped us understand the issues surrounding it.

We would like to thank our colleagues at the Association for Institutional Research for their leadership of this important book series, as well as series editor Larry Litten, who has been a supportive colleague and a diligent editor. We have developed a wonderful network of friends in the past year at Jossey-Bass Publishers, and in the endeavor to produce this volume, Jeff Wyneken provided us with another example of that organization's strength and capability.

The work of editing a volume such as this is hard but not nearly as hard as the work of authoring a unique and distinctive essay. The contributing authors of this volume are busy and accomplished leaders in higher education, who undertook this work in evenings and on weekends out of passion for their work and love for higher education. We can never thank them enough.

EDUCAUSE President Brian L. Hawkins and the board of directors of EDUCAUSE have shown steadfast commitment to providing leadership in higher education through the printed word. Under their leadership EDUCAUSE and its high-quality publications have placed an unmistakable accent on higher education's dialogues on a variety of complex issues.

The delivery of the EDUCAUSE mission depends in part on the generous and visionary leadership of corporate leaders. Such individuals and their firms share our deep respect for and commitment to higher education. SCT Education Systems has long been a partner of ours and a good friend of higher education. SCT's vision and commitment will make it possible for the IT leadership of nearly 1,700 colleges and universities worldwide to enjoy this volume and, we hope, in some small measure to learn from it. Thank you for your continued support.

CONTENTS

EDITORS' NOTES

Information technology is transforming colleges and universities and, in so doing, is challenging the traditional assumptions that underlie how these institutions may plan, finance, and govern themselves and how public-policy makers choose among policy alternatives for higher education. The dominant feature of information technologies, particularly data communications networks, is to remove or relax the hard boundaries created by time and space. Stock exchanges now operate on a global basis, twenty-four hours a day. Simple banking transactions have become independent of the customer's branch or the nine-to-five banking weekday. Catalogue merchants and others now sell nearly $3 billion of goods and services annually, twenty-four hours a day, over the World Wide Web. It is natural in this environment that some campus leaders and educational policymakers are heralding an era in which a postsecondary education can be delivered anytime, anywhere.

The potential of information technology (IT) to alter modes of teaching, learning, scholarship, and institutional services is already much in evidence. A 1996 CAUSE survey found that nearly 60 percent of traditional U.S. colleges and universities reported offering *distance education* options. The U.S. Department of Education forecasts that by 1999 more than 45 percent of total enrollees will be adult learners (see nces.ed.gov), and most analysts predict that adult learners will be the most likely to be attracted by technologically enhanced modes of instruction, which can be designed to accommodate their schedules and locations.

Institutional research comprehends the set of practices and techniques through which institutions of higher education collect, manage, analyze, and report information about themselves for a variety of purposes. Such purposes include quality control (for example, accreditation), budget control, program planning, workload management, governance, and marketing, to name a few. Well-focused and-managed institutional research organizations administer and provide the information that guides the actions and decisions of campus executives, trustees, and policymakers. Institutional research is typically the campus function that is responsible for supplying information to an institution's governments—information on which state, regional, and national educational policy is based. Such information forms the basis of intramural and extramural decisions about allocations of funds to support a variety of institutionally based research and instructional programs. Such information also influences public opinion about the priorities and performance of the academy and often guides public policy about essential matters such as the nature and scale of public subsidies—for example, financial aid for undergraduate instruction.

The institutional research function is, then, a critical one. It has also been a moderately stable one, reflecting the general stability of the colleges and universities it serves. However, current technological developments induce a vision of college and university education that is revolutionary. Martin Trow (1997), for example, accurately describes the implicit slogan of elite educations as "propinquity and synchronicity," that is, here and now. Indeed, the institutional research function has long been organized to collect, analyze, and report information about institutions' priorities and use of time- and place-specific resources.

The growing demand for so-called lifelong learning and the potential of information technologies to deliver such learning in new ways are also encouraging newcomers to the educational enterprise. As Trow puts it, "Information technology will cut its own channels, leading to the creation of institutions that differ from those of today, institutions where the weight of history does not condition and constrain information technology's use" (p. 294). In general such new educational suppliers have been outside the pale of the educational funding and the performance comparisons that institutional researchers support. These nontraditional organizations, typically unseen from the institutional research perspective, are potentially threatening to traditional institutions, for many of them boast new (and improved) cost structures, service levels, and learning results. Indeed, the existence of a growing nontraditional segment of higher education may "tilt the competitive playing field" and force "middle-of-the-road" nonselective institutions to adapt, particularly in their use of information technology (Massy, 1998).

In order to address the convergence of the new possibilities and new competition unleashed by technology, a new partnership must be forged between campus information technologists, institutional researchers, and campus leaders. As information technology cuts new channels, the question, framed by Stanley Chodorow (1995) and others, must become, How does IT change the way we organize, fund, and evaluate our institutions? The purpose of this volume is to stimulate a discussion among these parties on the nature of information systems, information services, and information itself in the transformational context in which we find ourselves.

The potential of information technology to alter the effects of time and place on students, faculty, and other members of the college or university community suggests a radical rethinking of the kinds of information that our institutions will need for organizing, funding, and evaluating themselves. For example, the foundational unit of analysis for much postsecondary instruction is the Carnegie credit. This measure is based fundamentally on time and is used extensively to determine student progress to degree completion (itself a time-based concept), student learning gains, faculty workload, financial aid, and other higher education activities. The widespread deployment of learning technologies will also likely challenge our methods of measuring and acting on student participation patterns. What effect, for example, does asynchronous instruction have on student enrollment census dates? How will institutions of the future calculate student full-time equivalencies and student-faculty ratios, measures that often determine funding and pricing decisions, for so-called distant learners?

Information technology is also forcing the creation of new roles. Accounting for information technology capital investments and for the expense of new media specialists, instructional technologists, courseware designers, and others will challenge our traditional methods of accounting and financial reporting. These challenges, in turn, will necessitate the creation of new kinds of institutional comparisons, performance indicators, and funding strategies. Will a nonfaculty courseware specialist's time be treated as an instructional expense or as an academic support expense?

As information technologies enable new modes of instructional delivery, faculty roles and faculty relationships to students, technologists, and others will likely change in significant ways. The current prevailing practices in institutional research have not yet been revised to anticipate these changes. Most important, the confluence of new technology-enhanced modes of instruction (for example, asynchronous, distance, or distributed) with competition from new suppliers will likely stimulate the unbundling, for pricing purposes, of instructional activities from the wide variety of student services that exist on present campuses. The failure to anticipate new information requirements, to develop the information systems that support such requirements, and to acquire and manage the new information will put traditional institutions at a serious disadvantage in competitive markets compared to providers whose learners do not desire or need expensive counseling, groundskeeping, housing, and other services. Finally, "information about methods of [instructional] delivery will become more important, if for no other reason than to serve as an aid in understanding variations between institutions and to support critical policy analyses concerning costs and effectiveness of different approaches to delivering educational services" (Jones, 1998, p. 13). This information will be particularly important as policymakers increasingly allow the market to determine the shape and function of higher education (Knight Higher Education Collaborative, 1998). Such a shift suggests the need for fundamentally different information and information systems and services and, again, a new partnership between technology providers and institutional researchers.

If the institutional research organization is responsible for the data and analysis on which institutional priorities are to be set, funded, and evaluated, it is essential that institutional researchers understand the specific context in which information technology investments are being made. Too often information technology costs are analyzed in a vacuum, answering such general queries as: What did the central campus technology organization spend this year versus last year? or, What did we spend on information technology compared to what our peer institutions spent? Although meaningful, these questions are incomplete and on occasion can foster antagonism between those who deliver information technologies and those who make use of them. The most important questions, and those addressed by the contributors to this volume, are normative and relate to this central analysis, How did we advance a particular institutional goal *through* our investment in information technology?

Susan J. Foster and David E. Hollowell make this point convincingly in their chapter, which deals with integrating information technology planning and funding at the institutional level. Providing a framework for integrating IT planning and budgeting at the physical, operational, and functional levels, they reinforce the importance of basing information technology plans on a knowledge of who needs and who provides the information or service and on an understanding of the expected outcomes or benefits of a planned service. Foster and Hollowell argue that to accomplish the desired level of integration, planning processes should be culturally derived or at least should be strongly informed by the institutional culture. They advocate inclusionary governance of campus IT planning processes and development of a consultative structure or framework that "fits the way the institution behaves, not the way IT behaves." In addition to providing specific advice regarding the membership and meeting frequency of campus IT planning advisory groups, the authors propose leadership, quality of resources, and quantity of resources as the constructs that are fundamental for planning and budgeting for information technologies on campus. Importantly, these authors distinguish between planning that is strategic and planning that is tactical. Owing to the risks inherent in managing information technologies, Foster and Hollowell stress that IT planning should "be at least as much, if not more, tactical than strategic . . . [but] always . . . closely aligned with the institution's mission and goals."

The volatility and ubiquity of information technology make its use, impact, and value particularly difficult to assess. Joan K. Lippincott describes and evaluates efforts sponsored by the Coalition for Networked Information (CNI) to assess the impact of investments in network infrastructure, services, and information on several institutions' teaching missions and administrative operations. Lippincott describes a fundamental conundrum. Colleges and universities are facing increased market pressures and public calls for accountability. At the same time, she says, many of the various institutional units that share responsibility for providing and assessing information about IT usage and performance have not been collaborating to develop common data collection methods or instruments. Lippincott describes a number of the dominant assessment models for network resources in use today and insightfully warns the would-be assessor to "make conscious decisions at the outset of the project regarding the purpose of the assessment and the audience for the results." This is an essential observation on the potential for much-needed partnerships between independent experts such as institutional researchers, librarians, information technologists, and faculty. Lippincott describes the deployment of assessment projects at one U.K. and six U.S. colleges and universities and provides frank and useful lessons learned from these projects to those contemplating meaningful assessment activity. In particular she reinforces the need for an engaged and active leadership that is involved in the process and that identifies assessment activity as an institutional priority. Her chapter concludes with guidelines that can greatly enhance any institution's efforts in the critical area of assessing the impact of campus networks.

The chapter that describes modeling the cost and quality of IT services at Indiana University bears witness to Kenneth C. Green's recent observation (1998) that colleges continue to struggle with IT planning. In this chapter Christopher Spalding Peebles, Laurie G. Antolovic, Norma B. Holland, Karen Hoeve Adams, Debby Allmayer, and Phyllis H. Davidson describe how frameworks for measuring costs, quality, and process performance that were pioneered in industry can be implemented successfully in an academic setting. Against the backdrop of growing customer demands, increasing complexity, static budgets, and shortages of skilled professionals, Indiana University's Information Technology Services has developed a rigorous regimen of customer satisfaction surveys and activity-based costing analysis to develop a performance scorecard that can guide organizational and investment decisions. In addition, Indiana University's Institute for Survey Research has, since 1990, conducted surveys of students, faculty, and staff to determine their information technology requirements and the extent to which these customers' needs had been addressed. The information generated through surveys and costing activities is used to inform IU's IT organization and strategy (an outcome that reinforces Hollowell and Foster's observations about the interplay between tactical information, organization, culture, and strategic planning). The authors describe their current efforts, building on this work, to assess the value of information technology to the campus, particularly in support of teaching and learning. In a powerful fashion this chapter balances a summary of the academic literature with a description of how these important analytical techniques were adapted for successful use in higher education. The authors' major findings are brought together in a detailed case study related to assessing the cost and quality of student computing on the IU Bloomington campus.

C. David Taylor and Joanne D. Eustis's chapter on assessing the impact of technology on teaching and learning at Virginia Tech addresses directly Martin Trow's haunting observation that "information technology is embedded in and used by institutions that have a history" (p. 294). The authors describe the pressing calls for increased accountability in the state of Virginia, the state mandate that higher education use information technology in its restructuring efforts, and the development and implementation of models to assess IT's contributions to instruction. These authors raise and deal with the most complex issue facing higher education's leaders: "How does an institution make decisions about new directions in course content and modes of learning within a shared governance system and a community with diverse values and agendas?" Taylor and Eustis describe how an ad hoc multidisciplinary group of faculty proceeded to "test the efficacy and push the limits of computer-mediated communication technologies." The institution drew ideas and inspiration from this group, eventually winning substantial foundation funding to explore the application of asynchronous learning networks at Virginia Tech. A major condition of this external support was that the funded project emphasize evaluation and assessment. In particular, Virginia Tech implemented techniques to assess such key issues as the nature of self-paced learning in large, mixed-ability classes; the role of technology in relieving faculty of repetitive tasks; and the impact of information technology on learning, motivation, and student success. Recently, the Center for Innovation in Learning was created to "integrate research on teaching and learning into the curriculum" and to evaluate "new, technology-based teaching and learning approaches." The authors describe in detail the set of qualitative and quantitative methods being used and continually refined at Virginia Tech to assess IT's various impacts, including the institution's involvement in national assessment studies and projects.

In this volume's final chapter, Gerald Bernbom discusses the institution's responsibility to manage its own information. Bernbom reminds us that the value of information technology depends ultimately on the role and use of information in organizations. He suggests the need for institutions to begin to assess their own practices relating to how information is created and protected, how and by whom it is used, how information is valued, and how the value of institutional information is affected by its timeliness, accuracy, and accessibility. Bernbom eschews the scholarly record in favor of a focus on administrative data, enterprise data, management information, and institutional records and argues convincingly for the adoption of an institution-wide view of information. Owing to organizational and communications fragmentation or to the proliferation of legacy and shadow systems, an institution's data, records, and information are frequently fragmented. As a result, Bernbom says, data are collected, stored, and acted on multiple times at a cost of time and accuracy. This chapter describes "good information management" practices, a set of goals, guidelines, and techniques for promoting the effective and efficient use of the institution's information. Bernbom outlines the primary elements of these practices and suggests a number of assessment issues associated with each. He describes a powerful and useful framework for understanding the campus information environment, distinguishing between the uses to which an institution puts information *(information architecture)*, the rules and guidelines that the institution develops to structure its information management activities *(information policy)*, and the set of practices and priorities with which the institution seeks to preserve and enhance the value of information *(data administration)*. His views bring together the common interests of campus technologists, institutional researchers, archivists, records managers, and librarians with those of the creators and users of institutional information.

In sum, the contributors to this volume conclude, not surprisingly, that information technology is changing dramatically the ways traditional colleges and universities are delivering their missions. These changes in turn will suggest new ways of organizing, funding, and assessing programs and services. Some of the changes fostered by information technologies will necessitate a reexamination of fundamental approaches to institutional planning and budgeting and hence to institutional resources. In particular, programs unbundled from the campus will need to be measured, assessed, and funded in new ways.

To harness these changes to best effect, institutions are advised to align their information technology plans closely with their goals for teaching, learning, scholarship, and service. In particular, a closer relationship between institutional researchers and information technologists must be forged to ensure that institutional information is managed responsibly, efficiently, and effectively and to develop shared understandings of how IT investments should be made, measured, and assessed. The largely quantitative analytical strengths of the institutional research organization should be brought to bear on the assessment of IT's contributions to the campus mission and should be supplemented with a commitment to qualitative assessments of service and user expectations and perceptions.

The stakes in higher education's changing game are big enough to demand new levels of collaboration among those responsible for creating, managing, using, analyzing, and reporting an institution's priorities, behaviors, and investments. Such collaboration might particularly include faculty, students, institutional researchers, information technologists, librarians, and records managers.

Finally, as in all things, leadership does matter. The story of planning and assessing information technology in higher education is a story about change. Change demands a clear vision and a campuswide commitment to using information technologies in ways that reinforce this vision and the goals associated with it. It will be prudent to assume that information technology can make a positive difference to the campus community and to test, evaluate, and assess this assumption regularly!

Richard N. Katz
Julia A. Rudy
Editors

References

Chodorow, S. "Educators Must Take the Electronic Revolution Seriously." Alan Gregg Memorial Lecture, presented at the 106th Annual Meeting of the American Association of Medical Colleges, Washington, D.C., Oct. 22–Nov. 2, 1995.

Green, K. C. *Colleges Struggle with IT Planning.* Claremont, Calif.: Campus Computing Project, 1998.

Jones, D. "New Institutional and Programmatic Configurations." In U.S. Department of Education, National Center for Education Statistics, *Technology and Its Ramifications for Data Systems: Report of the Policy Panel on Technology,* NCES 98-279. Washington, D.C.: U.S. Department of Education, 1998.

Knight Higher Education Collaborative. "A Very Public Agenda." *Pew Policy Perspectives,* Sept. 1998, 8 (2), 1–10.

Massy, W. F. "Understanding New Faculty Roles and Work Patterns." In U.S. Department of Education, National Center for Education Statistics, *Technology and Its Ramifications for*

Data Systems: Report of the Policy Panel on Technology, NCES 98-279. Washington, D.C.: U.S. Department of Education, 1998.

National Center for Education Statistics [nces.ed.gov].

Trow, M. "The Development of Information Technology in American Higher Education." *Daedalus,* 1997, *126* (4), 293–314.

RICHARD N. KATZ *is a vice president of EDUCAUSE, a nonprofit association dedicated to transforming education through information technologies.*

JULIA A. RUDY *is director of research and development and editor of the journal* CAUSE/EFFECT *at EDUCAUSE.*

Effective information technology planning cannot take place in a vacuum. It must be integrated into institutional planning, mission, and goals. This chapter examines key constructs for ensuring that the acquisition and implementation of information technologies furthers the institution's strategic plan. The authors recommend an inclusive governance structure and a facility planning approach, discuss funding alternatives, and address the role of institutional research in the IT planning process.

Integrating Information Technology Planning and Funding at the Institutional Level

Susan J. Foster, David E. Hollowell

By policy or practice, increasing numbers of colleges and universities are mandating the use of information technology (IT) to manage, teach, learn, do research, and reach out to their communities and the world. On most campuses, electronic mail is challenging the memorandum and the telephone as the primary means of remote communication, certain records are available only in electronic format, and libraries augment holdings of scholarly information with electronic databases and search services. Many institutions achieve, or expect to achieve, enhanced teaching and learning productivity (however they measure it) by using multimedia technologies in instruction. The research community relies increasingly on information technologies for scholarly communication, access to scholarly journals and databases, and access to large-scale, high-performance computing resources.

Whether consciously or not, we have come to make information technology an essential part of most of what we do. Ignoring the new need to make technology planning an integral part of institutional planning would be like ignoring the traditional need to plan for space, library holdings, and staffing when deciding to implement a new academic program. As campuses plan their futures the infrastructure necessary for access to information and the recurring costs associated with keeping current with technology must be considered.

Effective information technology planning does not take place in a vacuum. It must be integrated into institutional planning, mission, and goals. At the physical level it must be an integral part of every construction and renovation endeavor. At the operational level it must meet demand for access to IT resources. At the functional level it must serve the institution's community: students, faculty, researchers, administrators, prospective students and employees, alumni, and parents—all those who endeavor to acquire, create, and convey knowledge.

Catalysts for integrated IT planning include a well-informed executive management, high visibility of the essential value of information technologies to institutional goals and objectives, and a broadly based understanding that information technologies serve at three levels: the physical, or transport, infrastructure (cable and network electronics); the logical, or intelligent, infrastructure (servers and software); and the application, or usable, infrastructure (information resources, management, and support).

Facility planners will not build a new building or even recommend one without understanding who is to use it, for what end they are to use it, and what the users need to achieve their objectives. Essentials such as electrical service; plumbing; and heating, ventilating, and air-conditioning (HVAC) will not be left out of the equation. Traffic flows, room sizes, equipment, and materials will be designed with the specific needs of the occupants in mind. Well-accepted methods help facilities planners arrive at accurate power, water, and HVAC requirements for any environment for which all the relevant attributes are known.

Effective information technology planning is similarly achievable. What are the relevant attributes that must be known in order to achieve effective IT planning and develop information technologies strategically? We need to know who is using and who is providing the information or service. We need to know the nature of the information or service. And we need to know what outcomes or benefits are expected.

Inclusive IT Governance

Plans for curriculum development, management services, research, and outreach all need to take information technologies into account. Integrated IT planning is most successful when it is inclusive. Faculty, department heads, deans, and other administrators need to understand and embrace the role of information technologies in achieving their institution's mission and goals. IT planners need to learn each group's requirements for usability and access, the outcomes the group is expecting, how outcomes will be measured, and how costs will be weighed against outcomes achieved.

Effective IT planning is best achieved in an institutional culture that encourages and expects consultation and collaboration within and in an organization that has permeable internal boundaries. Regular communication through advisory and governance mechanisms and interaction between IT personnel and deans, directors, and other campus leaders encourage information flow and the application of strategic technologies. This continual push-pull exchange of needs and ideas also generates the energy that engages the creativity in all of us.

Each institutional culture produces its own governance structure, but we believe that the more inclusive the planning process, the more effective the results. A wide use of committees informs the planning process. Inclusive governance for IT plays an important role in maintaining communication, collaboration, and the permeability of internal boundaries.

It is important to understand the difference between governance and implementation. The role of governance is to establish policy and provide procedural advice. It is not to do the work. Work is handled best by groups drawn from project stakeholders and convened especially for the tasks at hand. IT organizations need governance primarily to remain close to their constituents, exchange useful information, and gain broad acceptance of their role. Institutions should not delegate IT responsibilities to governance bodies nor should those bodies assume those responsibilities.

IT without a governance structure is like government without sunshine laws. The value of IT is too great and the opportunities for ill-informed missteps too frequent for IT to be left without governance. The question does arise, however, How much governance is needed and how should it be structured? Though inclusive IT governance is sometimes criticized for appearing complex and too large, the fact is that it is less a hierarchy and more a matrix of groups with special foci. The key is to find the structure or framework that fits the way the institution behaves, not the way IT behaves (though there should be no difference between the two in a successful IT organization).

A group of administrators may work on the design of one-stop-shopping student services, for example, and a group of faculty may work on a set of recommendations to achieve a technology and service infrastructure to meet faculty needs. Faculty may emphasize the need to reduce institutional overhead by introducing technology wherever possible, though they may also worry about the capital cost of doing so in a time of tight resources. They may emphasize their requirements for a ubiquitous network infrastructure to prepare for the coming needs of teaching and research. They may establish requirements for departmental computing support and funding. They may outline their need for easier and broader access to scholarly material. They will almost certainly want to see these needs met in the shortest time possible.

Other groups may be called into existence to serve as advisory panels or task groups for various IT projects undertaken to meet the institution's mission and goals. A group of researchers may advise on the high-performance computation environment. A student life and faculty group may advise on the selection and use of programming for a campus television cable system. Another faculty group may advise on instructional needs. Yet another group may inform the Web site development process by establishing guidelines on use, appearance, and institutional image.

A broadly based group may be formed to search for a new financial system and recommend operational changes. Yet another group may be formed to select a new human resource system and to work on implementation and process reengineering.

It is important to note that all these task groups should be represented in the governance structure even as they come and go. The interests and work of these groups should be represented in one place, preferably a presidential committee made up of representatives from various other committees, vice presidential areas, the colleges, the students, and especially the institutional researchers and planners. This body should meet a limited number of times, say no more than five times a year, to share information, give their input on current IT initiatives, recommend policy, and produce a widely promulgated annual report.

Key Planning Constructs

Three constructs that are fundamental to planning and budgeting for information technologies are leadership, quality of resources, and quantity of resources.

Leadership. Visible, consistent leadership for information technology on campus is an important ingredient in achieving integrated IT planning. There are several ways to accomplish such visible leadership. One is for the institution's executive management to publicly recognize individuals and the value of IT. Another is to place the individual with overall responsibility for information technology in the highest ranks of the institution's management structure.

Though it is not currently the most common model, increasing numbers of campuses are moving toward an IT organizational structure that consolidates administrative and academic computing, telecommunications, network services, and instructional media services under a chief technology officer, commonly known as a chief information officer (CIO). This officer usually has ready access to the institution's decision makers and is as much a part of the executive management structure as institutional culture permits. Institutions that select this organizational model believe that this structure enhances their ability to optimize the use of resources and quickly seize opportunities to employ technology in new and creative ways.

With or without a CIO at its head, the IT organization itself must have positive visibility at all levels of the institution and with all constituencies. An IT organization's ability to be consistent, relevant, open, and inclusive determines the level of trust and success it will achieve.

Quality of Resources. The quality of information technology resources must be paramount in the planning process. Before embarking on any initiative it is important for planners to understand resource quality required at implementation, resource sustainability, and required resource reliability. Concern with the quality of information technology resources extends to the cabling and electronics, the software and servers, and the support and service. The questions to ask are: Will the resources meet demand? Are they reliable and supportable? Can they sustain growth? The answers will lead to an understanding of the required funding and staffing and of the life cycle of usability and maintenance.

Quantity of Resources. Information technology is a major consumer of resources. Planning for acquisition, enhancement, and replacement of IT resources must be an integral part of an institution's operating and capital budgeting process. Providing an IT infrastructure within an institution must be dealt with in the same way that supporting the library and providing and maintaining buildings and a utility infrastructure have been dealt with in the past. Members of our campus communities will come to expect (if they do not already) IT resources to be widely available and equal to demand. This result can be achieved only if the IT infrastructure requirements are properly considered in the institution's planning and budgeting process (Ringle and Updegrove, 1998).

Planning and Budgeting for IT

A common approach to strategic planning for IT in the past has been the development of a large, comprehensive document that spells out the institution's needs and the resources required to fulfill those needs. This is typically a *selling* document, used to prepare the institution for both the benefits and the costs. Although there is value in this approach, there is also risk. Emerging technologies can alter priorities and present unplanned but desirable opportunities not foreseen by the *strategic* document. Thus it is important for IT planning to be at least as much *tactical* as strategic (if not more so). Nevertheless IT planning must always be closely aligned with the institution's mission and goals as articulated in the institutional strategic plan, even though that alignment need not be necessarily spelled out through specific IT goals and objectives. For example, the University of Delaware's strategic plan includes these goals:

- Move and maintain faculty and staff pay scales to a level at or above those of a set of regional benchmark institutions—this is important to attracting and retaining the best and brightest faculty and staff.
- Increase and sustain the growth of the amount of financial assistance available to students—this is important to attracting and retaining the best and brightest students independent of their ability to pay the costs of a Delaware education.
- Invest in the physical plant so that deferred maintenance becomes scheduled maintenance—this is important to enhancing the learning and living environment and to attracting and retaining faculty, students, and staff.
- Seek opportunities to grow as a student-centered campus—this is important to attracting and retaining students as well as to producing graduates who will feel a greater satisfaction with and loyalty to the institution.

Clearly absent from this list is any mention of information technology. However, technology is a means, an enabler, for achieving the institution's strategic objectives. It may do this directly, as in the case when it significantly supports a student-centered environment on campus. Colleges and universities have typically not done a very good job of providing such basic administrative support services as registration, financial aid processing, and billing to students, but new, integrated, on-line student information systems not only help student services staff provide services more effectively and efficiently but also help students better serve themselves. Using the World Wide Web, institutions can actually replace, or at least minimize the need for, the physical student services center. With an electronic one-stop-shopping service, using Web-based technology that is available anytime from just about anywhere, students can register, obtain grades, change majors, monitor degree progress, use library services (including full-text electronic databases, electronic reserves, and on-line book renewal), and perform many other administrative functions.

These student-centered services usually do not materialize all at once but may appear rapidly one after another, as each new one has its demonstrated effect upon the next. Though it is tempting to say that this is an example of the build-it-and-they-will-come theory of technology deployment, it is much more accurate to say that it must be built *because they are coming*. A key to success is measuring the demand and being just in time with cost-effective technologies and support.

At other times IT's effect is more indirect, when, for example, it streamlines operations and achieves cost reductions in one area, allowing other areas to be addressed. In this regard an institution's leadership must understand technology's current and potential capability to reduce expenses, and expect that the efficient application of technology can free resources for reallocation to stated strategic objectives.

Infrastructure Planning. When technology is accepted as a means to achieving the strategic plan and as a vehicle for conducting university business, a tactical IT plan will include convenient access to technology and the resources it provides. One needs to think about access to the campus network like access to any other utility (electricity, heat, telephone). It is important to avoid the temptation to fall into a piecemeal approach that results in some departments having nonstandard networks and some having only as much service as they are able to afford rather than as much as they need. A central network services organization, guided by input from the campus as appropriate, needs to design the campuswide distribution system and to develop guidelines on how building and departmental subnetworks will interconnect with the campus network.

The network planning and implementation process should be directly parallel to the process campuses have used for years to centrally plan and support electrical distribution.

When planners are considering electrical distribution, intended uses of the space dictate the amount of service to be provided. If a building is made up primarily of office space, demand for electric service likely will be substantially less than demand in a building containing shops and laboratories.

Decisions are made about the size of the transformer, number of secondary distribution panels, and so forth based on such building use criteria.

Similarly, when planners consider the campus network infrastructure, they may find an office building needs a large number of connections but the volume and speed of data access needed is likely much different from that needed in a research building, which may require fewer connections but higher speeds and volume. This kind of analysis helps to determine the amount of optical fiber that must terminate in a building, how much service can be provided over copper wire, and the particular locations in the building that need both fiber and wire. As with electrical distribution, planners also arrange for some excess capacity and an in-building distribution method that is relatively easy to modify as needs change. The trade-off is always the cost to provide more now versus the cost of adding capacity later as needed.

Life Cycle Budgeting. Institutions need to develop life cycle funding plans for technology. Although technology changes on a very short cycle, the key question is how much change the institution can let go by before its failure to upgrade inhibits the educational process or becomes a barrier to productivity. The Web provides a friendly user interface for collecting data and supplying information. However, efficient use of the Web and of an institution's intranet requires Pentium-level processors. A robust 486-level processor will do for the basics but not for long. Without the required level of technology the faculty, staff, and students cannot get an optimum level of service.

Establish a life cycle of three to four years for desktop equipment and budget accordingly. This includes departmental equipment obtained through gifts and grants for instruction or research. The institution must be clear about how timely replacement of departmental equipment will be planned and budgeted. A useful set of guidelines can go far to facilitate this process.

Funding Information Technology Investments

A direct and recurring infusion of capital funds for computing is essential. However, it is best if these are deployed tactically through an annual process. There are some items that may appear on the list every year, such as regular replacement of desktop computers for faculty and staff. However, what is allocated in one year for equipment to support research computing may well be allocated for network upgrades in the next. Again, note the close parallel to the commonly used process to determine the allocation of capital maintenance funds, which are budgeted typically as a lump sum and allocated annually based on needs and priorities at the time.

Redirecting Revenue Sources. Institutions can create or redirect revenue sources to support technology in order to avoid reallocating existing funds away from the academic mission. Two examples of other revenue sources are funds from student long distance telephone resale and savings from negotiating lower telecommunication costs for the campus as a whole.

In the case of student long distance telephone resale, an institution may be able to offer long distance service to students at a cost well below telephone credit card rates. Students save money, and the institution can realize a net revenue gain from matching times of student peak long distance use with times of low faculty and staff use. These funds may then be captured to support student access to the network or to maintain student computer laboratories with up-to-date equipment and software or both. With regard to lower telephone service rates (for both local and long distance services), an institution may decide to use a portion or all of the savings as a source of funds to support campus research and education network development and access.

Reallocating Resources from Operational Efficiencies. Other rich sources of resources for reallocation are process reengineering and automation. Most administrative procedures can be reviewed with the objective of simplifying them as much as possible and with an eye toward using technology as a substitute for rules-based tasks, numerous paper copies, and manual routing of documents. For example, in many institutions multiple signatures are required in routine form processing as a means of notification rather than for resource control. Electronic forms processing can easily eliminate these steps; providing electronic notification about a transaction to the appropriate parties is usually a satisfactory substitute for signatures.

Institutional procurement is another excellent example of a process in which labor- and paper-intensive procedures can be eliminated and the level of service increased. Order information can be captured once on an electronic form at the point of origination and then be handled electronically throughout the process. Electronic approvals can be attached to the electronic record. The procurement office can match orders to existing contracts or route orders to vendors via e-mail or computer-generated fax. Procurement can become a completely paperless process. A simple next step is to initiate a procurement card program that uses a Web-based system for account charge reconciliation, eliminating even more steps and paper. Savings in personnel and paper costs can be reallocated to more important endeavors even as the campus is being better served by its procurement office—a win-win situation.

Charging a Technology Fee. Some institutions, particularly those under close state control, may not have the flexibility to reallocate funds as just described. One solution for state-assisted institutions has been to use targeted fees to generate revenue, and many colleges and universities have now instituted computing or technology fees to assist with the costs of making computing resources available to students (Green, 1997). Although administrators often have differing views on the desirability of targeted fees in general, students themselves have often strongly supported technology fees because they recognize their need for exposure to current technology and demand the convenience and intellectual extension that IT can offer.

Determining How Much to Spend. How much should an institution spend on information technology compared to buildings, libraries, faculty, and other traditional needs? There is no simple answer to that question. For one thing, many institutions do not know how much they are spending campuswide because IT expenditures are made in so many different areas across an institution (Green and Jenkins, 1998). Lacking complete internal information and also lacking a common method for reporting institutional IT expenditures, institutions cannot easily use benchmarking to compare their costs against those of other institutions.

Moreover, there is no right answer to how much should be spent on buildings because this decision is driven by type, age, condition, and demand. There is no right answer to how much should be spent on libraries because this decision is driven by kinds of academic programs and by size and type of collection. So also there is no right answer to how much should be spent on technology. There are, however, ways to spend *well*, whatever the amount. The key is to be smart about technology expenditures—assess needs and apply resources to the highest priorities and in places where the returns will be greatest. Technology spending should be thought of as an *investment* in the physical and intellectual capital of the institution. If this sounds familiar, it should!

Is it possible to spend too much on technology? Absolutely! As in any other field, unwise and premature decisions can be made. Cost-benefit analyses need to be done whenever possible when investing in technology for administrative support. For example, at what point does it make sense to apply imaging technology to alumni and donor records? What does it cost to maintain records now? What will it cost to image these records? Is it important to image records retrospectively? What benefits or cost savings will accrue?

An example of an investment area that may be more difficult to quantify is research computing for faculty without grant support. Will adding X amount of capacity make it possible for Y number of faculty to develop concepts to the point where they can garner external support? To what extent does the teaching mission depend on faculty research that is neither externally funded nor, perhaps, externally fundable? These are complex questions that require input from the institution's policymakers, financial managers, deans, and faculty. In most cases the IT organization cannot do these analyses, though in some cases it may be able to lead them. Institutional research offices, however, can be of significant assistance in supplying and brokering the required information.

Institutional Research Roles

The institution's institutional research (IR) office should participate as much in planning and governance for information technology as it does in the overall institution-wide planning process. Although the functions within the role of the IR office may vary from campus to campus, a common function is recording and reporting institutional statistics, both internally and externally. The majority of these data are maintained in electronic form, in databases accessible through a variety of new tools. Institutional researchers must know where and how this information is kept and be facile with information technology tools so they can use and manage it. Institution research departments must be engaged in the IT planning process to ensure that the data provided meet the needs of those who rely on IT services.

IR departments are called upon regularly to measure outcomes and trends, usually in support of executive decision making. Without properly configured information resources and appropriate access, these tasks may be difficult and the validity of the results suspect. Therefore IR departments not only need to be included in the design of information systems but must be gatekeepers who monitor changes to definitions of data at the most elemental levels in order to ensure that such changes will not compromise later longitudinal analysis.

IR can offer valuable services to the IT organization in such areas as data warehousing, archiving, and refreshment cycles; user profiles; and data views. Moreover, like any other campus group, IT departments require good assessment tools to gauge technology needs and evaluate outcomes, and IR departments can be an excellent resource and expert partner for assessment techniques and tools. Like auditors, they can help develop for IT the much needed balanced view essential to successful planning and outcomes. (In Chapter Four of this volume, Taylor and Eustis elaborate on the role institutional researchers can play in assessing IT's impact on teaching and learning; in Chapter Five, Bernbom discusses in more detail IR's important role in institutional information management.)

Conclusion

In summary, a number of factors are critical to integrating IT planning and institutional planning and ensuring that technology investments are aligned with institutional mission and goals.

- A well-informed executive management and campuswide visibility for the essential value of information technologies to institutional goals and objectives
- Knowledge of who will use the technology, for what end they will use it, and what they will need to achieve their objectives
- Measurement of the demand and the ability to be just in time with cost-effective technologies and support
- A meaningfully functioning governance structure that fits the institution's culture
- Visible, consistent leadership for information technology and positive visibility for the IT organization
- Reliability, sustainability, and supportability of information technology resources
- Integration of the acquisition, enhancement, and replacement process for IT with the institution's operating and capital budgeting process
- Life cycle funding plans for technology and a direct and recurring infusion of capital funds for technology
- Participation of the institutional research department in IT planning and governance processes

References

Green, K. C. "Strategic and Financial Planning for Info Tech." Paper presented at CAUSE97, Orlando, Fla., Dec. 1997.

Green, K. C., and Jenkins, R. "IT Financial Planning 101: Developing an Institutional Strategy for Financing Technology." *Business Officer,* Mar. 1998, pp. 32–37.

Ringle, M., and Updegrove, D. "Is Strategic Planning for Technology an Oxymoron?" *CAUSE/EFFECT,* 1998, *21* (1), 18–23 [www.educause.edu/ir/library/html/cem9814.html].

SUSAN J. FOSTER is vice president for information technologies at the University of Delaware.

DAVID E. HOLLOWELL is executive vice president of the University of Delaware.

This chapter describes a project sponsored by the Coalition for Networked Information (CNI), which coordinated the work of seven higher education institutions as they conducted assessments of their campus networks and networked information. It offers background on the climate of networking on campuses, explores why assessment is currently necessary, briefly overviews some information technology assessment efforts under way in higher education, describes the specific campus initiatives of the CNI project, and discusses lessons learned from these initiatives.

Assessing the Academic Networked Environment

Joan K. Lippincott

With the rapid expansion of the Internet, colleges and universities have been investing heavily in network infrastructure, equipment, services, and networked information resources. Such heavy investment is increasingly raising questions about the impact of information technology (IT) on an institution's teaching mission and administration. This chapter examines approaches some institutions have taken to assessing network services and networked information as part of a project sponsored by the Coalition for Networked Information.

The Coalition for Networked Information (CNI) was founded in 1990 to advance the interests of scholarship in the networked computer environment. Founded by a library association, the Association of Research Libraries (ARL), and two higher education computing associations, CAUSE and Educom (now consolidated into one association, EDUCAUSE), CNI brought together the content and service expertise of librarians with the networking and infrastructure expertise of information technologists. Higher education institutions formed the core of members, but early in the life of the CNI Task Force, many other types of organizations joined it. These organizations now number about two hundred and include publishers, hardware companies, network service

---

Christopher Peebles, associate vice president for research and academic computing, Indiana University, was a visiting fellow with CNI for the project described in this chapter and served with the author as a project coordinator. Charles McClure served as an advisor. Gerald Bernbom, special assistant for digital libraries and distance education, Indiana University, served as project facilitator. Samuel McDonald, a graduate student at Indiana University, provided project support. More information on CNI's Assessing the Academic Networked Environment project and also reports and instruments from the participating individual institutions can be found at www.cni.org/projects/assessing.

providers, scholarly associations, public and state libraries, and library consortia.

The coalition accomplishes some of its work through projects undertaken by institutions interested in focusing resources (staff time, equipment, funds) on a particular area of networks or networked information. CNI staff, along with leaders from the membership, identify and propose an initiative and issue an open call for participation, posted on CNI's news listserv and on its Web site (www.cni.org). Institutions that wish to participate in the project respond to the call, and generally about six to ten of them are selected, based on the criteria outlined in the call for participation. For each project, CNI seeks a diverse set of institutions, looking at factors including size, type (public or private), and geographical location.

In the call for participation for most institution-based projects, CNI places a particular emphasis on the use of cross-functional teams to carry out the work of the project. As an organization founded by librarians and information technologists working in partnership, CNI intends, as one aspect of its mission, to promote collaboration among various units of a higher education institution in the implementation of network and networked information projects. Institutional teams have worked on such CNI topics as university presses, networked theses and dissertations, and new learning communities. The CNI philosophy is that network and networked information projects require the participation of many sectors of the higher education institutions in which they are developed. Units such as the library, computing center, and instructional technology group cannot successfully operate in *silos*, developing services and solutions in isolation from each other and their potential users.

CNI's role in the projects it initiates is to develop the conceptualization and framework of the project, solicit participating institutions, organize and hold one or more meetings of the participating institutional teams, provide network services for the project, offer advice and counsel to participating teams, and provide a forum for the dissemination of project outcomes, through conference presentations and Web-based publications.

CNI was set up to be more agile and responsive than a typical association. There are no standing committees nor long approval processes for the development of new projects. The founding associations wanted CNI to be able to move into appropriate areas in the rapidly changing networked environment as quickly as possible.

Assessing the Academic Networked Environment

Networks and networked information services have been developing rapidly on campuses since the 1980s. Large research universities pioneered the development of the Internet, and by the mid-1990s, higher education institutions of all sizes were making significant use of the Internet for teaching and learning, research, marketing, and outreach. Campuses have made huge investments in networking infrastructure, in hardware and software, in facilities such as computer labs and classrooms, in services to support users, and in networked information resources, such as subscriptions to electronic databases and journals. However, if one attempts to collect information on the amount of money a given campus has spent to wire its physical plant, that information is generally not available. Often the wiring took place over many years, came from many budget sources, and the information was not consolidated and tracked by any campus unit.

Most institutions are also not collecting information on cost or amount of user support, which can include such activities as supplying help desks in computer labs, managing and staffing those labs, managing classroom facilities, conducting user workshops, developing electronic databases of answers to common questions to be used by help desk staff or directly by users, and offering in-depth consulting at a computing facility or a library reference desk.

One reason collecting such information is difficult is that in many cases a variety of institutional units have responsibility, and they generally have not collaborated to develop common data collection methods or instruments. For example, several units might conduct faculty workshops related to networking: the computer center might offer classes on accessing the campus network from home offices, the library might offer classes on using subject databases and other electronic information resources, and the instructional technology unit might offer workshops on using the World Wide Web effectively in classroom instruction.

Universities and colleges, particularly in the public sector, have come under increased scrutiny by boards of trustees, state legislators, and others in recent years. On campus some faculty complain about the funding going into computing and networking and away from other cherished programs. The need for accountability to the campus community and to influential outsiders is increasingly apparent, and too often when questions are asked about networking costs, impact, and use, no one can give answers because the data are not available.

Many aspects of the networked environment are potential topics for assessment: *networks* (the wiring infrastructure that includes local area networks, campus networks, and connections to the Internet as well as the equipment that supports those networks), *network services* (activities ranging from answering users' questions, providing training, and staffing computer labs and classrooms to developing Web sites for institutional or curricular needs), and *networked information resources* (digital information such as databases, electronic journals, and Web sites).

Overview of Assessment Efforts

Assessment of network services and availability and use of networked information on campuses was the focus of extensive research conducted by Charles McClure, distinguished professor at Syracuse University. His work identified five elements in the campus network: the technical infrastructure, content, services, support, and management. McClure noted with concern that the survey of campuses conducted as part of this research revealed a surprising dearth of programs and instruments for assessing the networked environment. Many of the individuals with whom he spoke felt that such assessment was an impossible task. McClure's work culminated in the publication by CNI of the manual *Assessing the Academic Networked Environment: Strategies and Options* (McClure and Lopata, 1996 [also available on-line; see the references]). The manual provides an overview of techniques with which institutions can conduct assessments of various aspects of networking on campus, and it includes sample instruments that can be used as a starting point.

In addition to McClure's work, some efforts have been made by individual institutions and associations to bring some structure to the assessment of networks, network services, and networked information resources.

The Higher Education Information Resources Alliance (HEIRAlliance), originally an alliance of CAUSE and Educom with the Association of Research Libraries and now an alliance of EDUCAUSE and ARL, produced guidelines on evaluation of institutional information resources in 1995 that provide an institution-wide perspective and an approach that emphasizes institutional planning. This document (on the Web at www.educause.edu/collab/heirapapers/hei2000.html) can be a useful framework for initial discussions on campus about appropriate areas and priorities for network assessment.

K. C. Green has conducted a survey of campus computer activity and published the results annually for the past eight years (see www.campuscomputing.net). His *Campus Computing Survey* provides a useful general sense of the degree of implementation and use of computing on campuses. Some topics for which he collects data are the use of specific technologies in instruction, the use of Internet resources in classes, and technology fees. Green surveys 605 two- and four-year colleges to compile his data.

CAUSE captured data about information technology hardware, software, organization, budget, personnel, policies, and so forth on its member campuses for nearly twenty years. These data were made available through custom reports to the association's members, and occasional reports summarizing survey data have been issued through the years. EDUCAUSE is in the process of evaluating this data collection program to make it more effective and responsive to institutional needs in the future.

The assessment work at Indiana University (IU), spearheaded by Christopher Peebles and described in Chapter Three, is a model program that addresses user satisfaction with computing services and also provides figures on costs for the services of University Information Technology Services (UITS), the central information technology organization at Indiana. UITS is not the only organization nor IU the only university to look at cost and quality of information technology. Karen Leach (Colgate University) and David Smallen (Hamilton College) have developed a national initiative for measurement and management of IT costs (Leach and Smallen, 1998) in which more than one hundred colleges and universities are participating.

The Association of Research Libraries has had a long-standing program of acquiring data from its members on such topics as library collections, expenditures, staffing, and services. A special issue of the *ARL Newsletter* (1998) on measures provides background on ARL's statistics program and also explores the newer territory of electronic information. Blixrud and Jewell (1998) report on ARL's recent attempts to collect data on its members' expenditures for electronic resources. ARL is working on resolving discrepancies in the interpretation of definitions used in the reporting of information about electronic resources and is helping institutions develop practical techniques to ensure accurate and consistent reporting. Although ARL and others have been addressing these issues since the early 1990s, the complexity of the situation, including new formats and new payment and licensing arrangements, precludes a quick development of a uniform mechanism for cross-institutional reporting of data on electronic resources.

One of the most ambitious and promising efforts in technology-related assessment is the Flashlight Project, directed by Stephen Ehrmann. Flashlight is a project of the TLT Group, a nonprofit firm that is the Teaching, Learning, and Technology Affiliate of the American Association for Higher Education. This project offers a variety of tools—survey instruments, interview questions, activity-based cost templates—designed for the assessment of information technology in teaching and learning at the postsecondary level. Background information about the Flashlight Project and an annotated bibliography for the study of teaching, learning, and technology can be found on the Web (www. tltgroup.org).

Another major seat of assessment activity was the Teaching and Learning Technology Support Network of the University of Glasgow, which conducted original research on the costs and benefits of information technology in higher education. This group also served as a point of collection for reports on information technology assessment from throughout Great Britain and the Commonwealth. Although this initiative ended in December 1998, a great variety of very high quality empirical and methodological papers can still be found on the group's Web site (www.elec.gla.ac.uk/TLTSN/index.html).

A working group of EDUCAUSE's National Learning Infrastructure Initiative, coconvened by the California State University (CSU) system and SHEEO (State Higher Education Executive Offices), has focused on developing a conceptual model to estimate the costs and benefits of various distributed instructional delivery modes and to compare them with the costs and benefits of classroom delivery. To carry out this effort the CSU received a two-year, $400,000 grant from the U.S. Department of Education to develop case studies in evaluating the benefits and costs of mediated instruction and distributed learning. The project, under the direction of Frank Jewett in the CSU Chancellor's Office, is developing a framework for cost and benefit identification and comparison, and also situational descriptions of a number of institutional cases that demonstrate different combinations of program goals, technology, and cost structures. Campus case studies are being reported as they become available at the project's Web site (www.calstate.edu/special_projects/mediated_instr).

Other research in the area of distance education costs and benefits has been reported by Bates (1995), Daniel (1996), and Rumble (1997). In addition, the University of British Columbia is nearing the end of a three-year project, under the direction of A. W. (Tony) Bates, studying costs and benefits of telelearning. The first case studies are now available on the Web at research.cstudies.ubc.ca/nce/index.html. The study is funded by the Canadian federal government and is part of the $1.3 million National Center of Excellence–Telelearning project headed by Linda Harasim and Tom Calvert at Simon Fraser University (Bates, 1998).

Also notable is the work being done at the Stanford Learning Laboratory (SLL) (sll-6.stanford.edu), established in 1997 to "enhance the learning experience of Stanford students and create a model for judicious use of pedagogically informed learning technology" (Sheppard and Marincovich, 1998). The SLL funded an assessment team of six core individuals and five advisers that worked with teaching and technology teams to define teaching and learning issues, goals, and questions that motivated the investment in Web technologies and to formulate an assessment plan to address the questions of the various stakeholders.

The networked environment is a risky environment in which there is much experimentation and constantly changing parameters. Professionals in many institutions are concerned that assessments of network services or network performance may reveal failures, user dissatisfactions, or total costs that would create controversy on campus. In developing network assessment projects, institutional teams must make conscious decisions at the outset about the purpose of the assessment and the audience for the results. If, for example, staff can be assured that the results of a user survey of the campus computer center help desk will be used internally by their unit to analyze and improve service, they will accept the survey more readily than they would if the results were slated to appear in the campus newspaper or on the president's desk.

CNI'S Assessment Project

After CNI published *Assessing the Academic Environment,* McClure asked the coalition to help him develop a program in which institutions would field test the measures the manual proposes and develop new measures for the academic networked environment. The manual consists of five sections: an overview; guidelines and suggestions for collecting qualitative data; measures designed to describe many factors in network use, services, and the impact of networking on campus activities; the employment of user surveys to assess the network; and a summary of the importance of ongoing assessment. The manual provided the framework for CNI's assessment project.

Project Scope and Participation. In the fall of 1996, CNI issued a call for participation in the assessment project, seeking institutions that were interested in doing network assessment projects on their campuses and sharing their results and lessons learned with others. Nine institutions were originally chosen to participate, but two dropped out at an early stage. The seven institutions that participated were a mix of large universities, small colleges, and one international institution: Brown University; Dartmouth College; Gettysburg College; King's College, London; Mary Washington College; University of Washington; and Virginia Polytechnic Institute and State University (Virginia Tech). The project was supported in part by a grant from the Council on Library and Information Resources.

Each institution selected one or more areas of networking or networked information to assess on its campus, focusing on issues of most concern to the institution. The areas included teaching and learning, help desk and support services, and library or other information services. The individual projects are described in the following sections. Each institution assembled a cross-sector team made up of individuals from departments such as the library, computing center, academic administration, and instructional design center. The teams all met at a CNI meeting in April of 1997 to launch the project. They discussed their local campus needs and were given overviews of assessment methodology. Each team also began to design its own assessment project.

The range of projects reported here reflects the wide influence and integration of networking on today's campuses and also provides evidence that institutions can identify specific issues, commensurate with institutional priorities and goals, that they can assess. Some of the projects focused very narrowly on one issue, and others were broadly conceived. Some proceeded smoothly, with adequate resources, support, and expertise, and others suffered from lack of administrative support, changes in staff, and tasks that turned out to be more time consuming and resource intensive than originally conceived. Many of the institutions dropped some aspect of their original assessment plan during the project as they lost staff or discovered how time consuming the efforts were. However, all the project team leaders reported satisfaction with some progress in the evolving area of assessing the academic networked environment. Only by beginning an assessment activity on campus can institutions make progress toward developing and refining measures that will be useful for units offering services and administrators and governing bodies seeking accountability.

Teaching and Learning. The University of Washington's UWired project is a model program that is infusing technology skills into existing curriculum and exploring opportunities for technology to facilitate teaching and learning. Components of the UWired program include the Center for Teaching, Learning and Technology; collaboratories; freshman interest groups; intercollegiate athletics; innovative courses; and outreach. Using a collaborative approach, UWired has developed evaluation plans for each component of its program. Some of the measurement techniques it has employed include paper-and-pencil questionnaires, Web-based questionnaires, e-mail questionnaires, and focus groups. UWired has worked on such assessment activities as helping the undergraduate education unit develop a new student survey that includes questions on computer and networked information use; tracking users of the Center for Teaching, Learning and Technology; and developing measures of the center's effect on teaching and learning. UWired personnel have been very successful in employing a team-based approach for many aspects of their project, including the assessment component. They have had the benefit of an individual with assessment expertise working closely with them as they develop measures. (Information about this project is also available from its Web site: www.washington.edu/uwired.)

At Mary Washington College a team of faculty and instructional technologists studied the expectations, experiences, and attitudes of both first-year faculty and first-year students in regard to the academic networked environment. Team members examined what computing experience the new faculty and students brought with them to campus, their expectations for using the academic network, and their attitudes toward the academic networked environment. Ayersman, Campbell, and Ackermann (1998) reported that one of their most interesting findings was the very different perceptions that faculty and students had of the use of e-mail for communication. Whereas 53 percent of the students anticipated using e-mail for communication, only 16 percent of faculty expected students to do so. Most students (73 percent) expected their instructors to communicate via e-mail to make assignments, answer questions, and provide class updates, but only 15 percent of the instructors anticipated doing so. The Mary Washington team collected its data through a background computing survey, a follow-up e-mail survey, and an attitudinal questionnaire. The team plans to convene focus groups of faculty and students to discuss differences and similarities in expectations toward using the network. The study establishes a baseline that will influence computing support and instructional plans on the campus. (See inte.mwc.edu/projects/cni/index.html for more information.)

Brown University developed an assessment of its training activities. Many computer centers and libraries offer stand-alone workshops and training sessions for learning various software packages, using e-mail, developing Web pages, and acquiring skills in other information technology areas. At Brown, Computing Center personnel analyzed some existing forms and measures that were used in their training program and critiqued their value. Existing in-class evaluations by class participants and an instructor feedback form provided useful information that personnel used to revise the content and nature of training sessions, but those instruments did not address the impact of the training sessions on users. The center developed a postcourse evaluation form to be sent via electronic mail to class participants two to four weeks after their training session. This timing was intended to allow users to apply what they had learned in the training session and get a more accurate picture of the value and impact of the session before completing the evaluation. Staff have found that these postcourse evaluations provide useful measures of the effectiveness of their training programs and help the computing training staff determine how effective the programs are in meeting the needs of various constituencies—staff, faculty, undergraduate students, and graduate students.

Virginia Tech's project involving teaching and learning is reported in depth in Chapter Four. Its ACCESS project, funded by an Alfred P. Sloan Foundation grant, examines issues and critical success factors in the use of technology in instruction.

Help Desk and Support Services. Dartmouth College Computing Services identifies the help desk as a critical point of interaction between the department and the user community. The greatly increasing demands on college and university campuses for technology support services and the deterioration in service quality have been documented by McClure, Smith, and Sitko (1997). Two considerations influenced the decision to assess this particular area of user support. The computing center and the library are developing a new facility in which they will jointly offer services to the user community. They hoped this study would help them understand user requirements and priorities that would assist them in designing the facility's physical layout and equipment. They also hoped the results would help Dartmouth decide whether it should move from centralized computing support to the distributed model being adopted on many campuses.

Dartmouth College conducted a two-phase assessment of its help desk service. In the first component, staff logged e-mail, walk-in, and phone consultations over a six-week period, recording the nature and characteristics of each interaction. In the second phase of the study a sample of the individuals who had used the service was interviewed by phone.

Among the things the Computing Services staff learned from their assessment were these:

- Overall, users find that the help desk is a good resource.
- Computing Services needs to be "smarter" and more efficient in its operations.
- Computing Services needs to put more resources into staff training.
- Users want one-stop shopping for problems with hardware, software, and the network (this finding has important implications for the development of the new facility with the library).
- Working with an institutional research professional was very useful in the design and implementation of the assessment; it was money well spent.

At Brown University, Computing Center staff identified improvement of services and institutional accountability as the goals for the help desk piece of their assessment project. They then identified six help desk assessment areas: question content, use by academic departments, telephone trends, turnaround time, customer satisfaction with quality of service, and customer satisfaction with the kinds of services offered.

For many of these issues, staff were able to gather data using Action Request software (from Remedy Corporation), which they were already using to solve difficult problems. Consultants entered data into the system and were able to generate reports on what software was most heavily used, which departments were using their services most heavily, the amount of time spent on requests, and other issues. In addition, the staff used telephone interviews and focus groups to ascertain customer satisfaction.

Library and Information Resources. Although many people think of Internet information resources as being available without charge, an increasing number of electronic information resources are being made available on the Internet on a fee basis, usually by subscription. Many of these resources were available to libraries and library users in electronic form prior to the widespread use of the Internet; the database *Chemical Abstracts* is an example. As publishing companies became aware of the impact of the Internet, first on higher education institutions and then on the public at large, they began to move electronic information products into the Internet environment. Academic libraries of all sizes now offer these products on a variety of platforms, such as CD-ROM, the campus mainframe, and the Internet.

Colleges and universities, generally through their libraries, are now paying substantial fees to license access to electronic information products on behalf of their users. In many cases the libraries also maintain subscriptions to the printed counterpart of the electronic resource. They do so for several reasons. First, their licensing agreement with the publisher may not give them the contractual right to preserve the electronic version far into the future. A library's role in part is to preserve the scholarly record for future generations, and its best guarantee at this point is to have that record on paper or microform. Proven technologies for long-term preservation of electronic information do not yet exist. Second, many users demand that the library maintain the print subscription even as other users lobby for access to the electronic version. The library tries to fulfill a variety of individual needs by maintaining dual subscriptions. However, few academic libraries have made concerted assessments of the use of electronic information products and user satisfaction or of the nature of the use of print versus on-line products when both formats exist. Access to scholarly information is an integral part both of teaching and learning and of research in the academic environment, and it is becoming increasingly costly to provide all the materials desired by the academic community.

At the University of Washington, library staff are redesigning their triennial library use survey to learn about use of networked information. In addition, staff conducted focus group sessions with faculty and graduate students in the biological sciences to determine how they are using information for their research and teaching activities. Staff asked group participants to describe how they identify, obtain, and use information for these activities. In addition, staff asked how the faculty and students would ideally like to get the information they need and why, how they used electronic journals, and what trade-offs they associated with this use.

At Virginia Tech the library participated in the development of a student survey designed by a number of campus units. Some of the questions the library added to the survey asked about students' use of links on the library's main Web page, use of the electronic reserve system, use of Virginia Tech and consortial catalogues, and use of databases and electronic journals. In addition, the library studied Web log data to determine where users were located when they connected to the library's Web page. They determined that fewer than half were actually inside the library building; most were using connections from dorm rooms, offices, or off-campus locations. This realization confirmed that the vision of an anytime, anyplace virtual library is important to users. The data also made librarians aware that they need to take remote users into account in their planning for services; for example, users who are not physically in the library cannot come to the reference desk when they have a question and get a quick response. Libraries are in only the preliminary stages of planning and implementing services to off-site users.

At Gettysburg College the assessment project focused on the use of and satisfaction with an electronic reserves system, developed on campus as part of the broader Curriculum Navigation project that provides a central source of information for the campus. In a collaboration between the library and the computing center, Gettysburg assessed why students used or did not use the electronic reserves system, determined usage patterns, and examined faculty and student satisfaction with the system. Consistent with the pattern at Virginia Tech, the Gettysburg findings showed that over half of the students using the electronic reserves accessed the system from outside the library building, largely from their dorms. Responses from faculty who used electronic reserves in their courses were particularly positive. They liked the statistical reports generated by the system, which identified how many individual students had accessed each item, and they felt that the ability of several students to access materials simultaneously over the network improved service.

At King's College, London, librarians working with information technologists are gathering data by electronic means when possible in their assessment project. They are looking at the use, cost per transaction/user, usage profiles, and system availability of electronic journals. King's College participates in a program for all U.K. universities that makes a large number of electronic resources available to users via a network. In making this heavy investment in electronic resources, King's wants to know if those investments are paying off for users. King's College is also examining the use of electronic versus printed information by department, document availability, and cost per item/user. In addition to these quantitative data, it is collecting qualitative data on the reasons users choose either print or electronic information, user preference, user satisfaction, and ease of administration.

A Role for Institutional Research

Institutional research professionals can play a useful assessment role by participating on cross-sector teams charged with planning assessment of the campus network environment. They can help the team clarify goals that relate to overall institutional objectives, such as assessing the infrastructure for distance education or developing and offering scholarly networked information resources. They can also help with basic definitions of terms (helping determine what constitutes a *user,* for example), so that assessment terms will be consonant with the ones used by the institutional research unit in other aspects of institutional measurement, such as counting students. And they can advise the team on appropriate methodologies for particular types of assessment and assist with the development of data collection instruments.

Although many institutions have technology plans, most do not follow through and evaluate whether those plans have been carried out and whether the plans have produced user satisfaction, the ultimate goal. Institutional researchers can work with campus information professionals to include performance measures and assessment techniques in technology plans.

Institutional researchers can also help compare campus networking trends to other institutional trends. For example, is the percentage of the campus budget allocated to networking increasing or decreasing at the same rate as the overall campus budget? Is the growing use of the network attributable to a growing student population rather than to increasing use by each student? Are student demographics changing, and if so, what implications might the changes have for the development and delivery of networks and networked information services? For example, if increasing numbers of students are living off campus, access to the network from outside the physical campus becomes a pressing issue. An area of particular importance in planning for the campus is the development of new facilities and the renovation of existing buildings. Institutional researchers, facilities planners, and information professionals can work together closely in this area to bring the campus into the information age.

Looking beyond the institution's boundaries, institutional researchers can help those who deliver network services to understand the environmental trends affecting higher education institutions and how these trends might have specific impacts on networking—for example, how state funding of higher education is affecting the institution, or how trends in distance education will affect it. They can also assist national groups in developing a framework for cross-institutional comparison of networks, network services, and networked information resources.

Lessons Learned

The institutional projects in CNI's Assessing the Academic Networked Environment project resulted in some very useful data for the institutions involved, provided examples for the higher education community at large, and marked some significant progress in recognition of the need for assessment in these areas. However, the projects also provided lessons on what can go wrong and on the difficulties of breaking new ground in assessing technologies and services that are developing and changing rapidly.

In choosing participating institutions for its projects, CNI attempts to identify institutional goals that are aligned with the project; these goals might exist, for example, when a campus president has identified developing assessment activities as a priority. This alignment proved to be a significant factor for another critical element of assessment, namely administrative support of the project. This support could be at the unit or department level, college level, or highest university level. It usually went hand-in-hand with identification of assessment as an institutional priority, and it was a factor in the success of many of the CNI projects. In those institutions where administrative support was not forthcoming, assessment projects were often considerably scaled back from original plans, and in one case an institution dropped its participation.

The time consumed by initiating assessment activities was also a factor in what the institutions accomplished. Once measures are in place and are part of a unit's operation, the amount of time needed for an assessment activity diminishes. However, the planning phase requires much time, often from a number of people. In implementing assessment techniques many look to automated data collection as a potential time-saving device. This can be true for the generation of quantitative data, but for qualitative measures such as Web-based surveys on attitudes, significant human involvement is still necessary.

Changes in staff and loss of staff also impeded the progress of some of the institutions' assessment initiatives. In most higher education institutions, computing and library staff numbers have remained small or even decreased as user demand for services has grown. Loss of a key individual in some aspect of the assessment initiative meant dropping that area from the CNI project for several institutions. Once measures for a particular area are developed, implemented, and refined, assessment should be less dependent on individual staff members. Institutions may want to consider adopting an understudy approach to staffing assessment projects.

Some of the institutions that participated in the CNI project were more successful in mounting collaborative efforts than others. In the networked environment an institution-wide view is important because many units often are working in the same area. Teamwork requires skills that may not be inherently available in the institutional units. As they develop their initiatives, assessment teams may want to consider participating in a professional development program that teaches teamwork and collaboration skills.

Exhibit 2.1 summarizes some key lessons learned as guidelines for network and networked information assessment.

The participating institutions in the CNI project are pioneers in assessing the academic networked environment. Their energy, enthusiasm, and thoughtfulness enriched the project and will provide a much wider audience with access to their experience.

Exhibit 2.1. Guidelines for Assessing the Impact of Campus Networks

- Bring together a network assessment team of individuals who are from various units on campus and who can add useful perspectives and expertise; include, if possible, someone who specializes in assessment.
- Align the overall goals of the network assessment initiative with the institution's goals and priorities.
- Gain support from the administration at as many levels as possible.
- Make a realistic determination of the resources (staff, time, equipment, money) available for the assessment.
- Choose a manageable assessment project as the first implementation; do not attempt a comprehensive assessment of campus networking on your first try.
- Consider using more than one assessment technique to measure the aspect of networking you have chosen; particularly consider combining quantitative and qualitative approaches as complementary techniques.
- Identify carefully the audience(s) for the assessment report(s).
- Examine what you might do with the information you collect (improve services, seek additional funding) and determine whether your data will be relevant to reaching that objective.
- Refine assessment instruments periodically and add new components incrementally.
- Monitor the work of national groups such as ARL, EDUCAUSE, CNI, and the Flashlight Project to see whether materials they develop and guidelines they produce can provide a framework for your project.

References

ARL Newsletter, 1998, 197 (special issue), 1–20.

Ayersman, D. J., Campbell, G., and Ackermann, E. "Expectations, Experiences, and Attitudes of First-Year Faculty and Students Relative to the Academic Networked Environment." Paper presented at the International ED-MEDIA Conference, Freiburg, Germany, June 1998.

Bates, A. W. Technology, Open Learning and Distance Education. New York: Routledge, 1995.

Bates, A. W. Readers Respond Department. CAUSE/EFFECT, 1998, 21 (2), 62–64. [www.educause.edu/ir/library/html/cem982d.html].

Blixrud, J. C., and Jewell, T. D. "Understanding Electronic Resources and Library Materials Expenditures: An Incomplete Picture." ARL Newsletter, 1998, 197 (special issue), 12–13.

Daniel, J. S. Mega-Universities and Knowledge Media. London: Kogan Page, 1996.

Higher Education Information Resources Alliance (HEIRAlliance). Evaluation Guidelines for Institutional Information Resources. Boulder, Colo.: CAUSE, 1995. [www.educause.edu/collab/heirapapers/hei2000.html].

Leach, K., and Smallen, D. L. "What Do Information Technology Support Services Really Cost?" CAUSE/EFFECT, 1998, 21 (2), 38–45. [www.educause.edu/ir/library/html/cem9829.html].

McClure, C. R., and Lopata, C. L. Assessing the Academic Networked Environment: Strategies and Options. Washington, D.C.: Coalition for Networked Information, 1996. [www.cni.org/projects/assessing].

McClure, P. A., Smith, J. W., and Sitko, T. D. The Crisis in Information Technology Support: Has Our Current Model Reached Its Limit? CAUSE Professional Paper, no. 16. Boulder, Colo.: CAUSE, 1997. [www.educause.edu/ir/library/html/pub3016/16index.html].

Rumble, G. The Costs and Economics of Open and Distance Learning. London: Kogan Page, 1997.

Sheppard, S., and Marincovich, M. Readers Respond Department. CAUSE/EFFECT, 1998, 21 (2), 62–64. [www.educause.edu/ir/library/html/cem982d.html].

JOAN K. LIPPINCOTT is associate executive director of the Coalition for Networked Information, a joint program of the Association of Research Libraries and EDU-CAUSE.

*In an era of ever more constrained resources and vastly increased
demand for services, the performance of college and university
information technology organizations has been questioned relentlessly
by faculty, students, and administrators. This chapter describes three
families of measures—quality, cost, and value—that can answer such
questions, at least in part, and can turn the discussion from one of
conflicting opinions to one of critical and productive dialogue and
change.*

Modeling and Managing the Cost and Quality of Information Technology Services at Indiana University: A Case Study

*Christopher Spalding Peebles, Laurie G. Antolovic,
Norma B. Holland, Karen Hoeve Adams, Debby Allmayer,
Phyllis H. Davidson*

Chief information officers (CIOs), whether in universities or in industry, have
much in common with Alice in Lewis Carroll's *Through the Looking-Glass.* They
would feel considerable empathy for Alice in her mad rush through the Garden
of Living Flowers, the one in which she got nowhere, despite her best
efforts. The Red Queen explains to Alice that her lack of progress was to be
expected: "Now *here,* you see, it takes all the running *you* can do to keep in the
same place. If you want to get somewhere else you must run at least twice as
fast as that!" (Carroll, [1897] 1992, p. 127).

The notion of working hard just to stay in the same place has been taken
up by the biological sciences to describe the origin, persistence, and evolution
of species and has been termed the *Red Queen Hypothesis.* This metaphor can
also be applied to the operation and development of formal organizations
in competitive environments, especially information technology organizations, because it certainly is descriptive of the challenges they face and their
successful responses in the last two or three decades. For academic information technology (IT) organizations, constrained as they are by more or
less fixed budgets, the pressure to run harder comes from several directions
simultaneously.

First, the number of users for IT services has increased. At Indiana University (IU) those who use IT services have gone from a few hundred to over one hundred thousand in little more than a decade.

Second, the complexity of the computing environment in both the private and public sectors has increased. At IU we have gone from a couple of mainframes and operating systems to a bewildering variety of desktop and laptop machines, five major operating systems, five variants of UNIX, at least three client-server configurations, and the old standby mainframe is still with us.

Third, the applications users demand have gone from a few to a few hundred. At IU fewer than one hundred are used habitually, but the variety within that one hundred is great nonetheless.

Fourth, the networking and regulatory environments have become technically and semiotically grotesque. Plain old telephone services (POTS) and the old reliable and tractable System Network Architecture (SNA) have been displaced by internets, intranets, wide area networks (WANs), local area networks (LANs), wireless technology, digital video on demand, and something known as voice over IP. At IU, as elsewhere, IT organizations are being overtaken by the *convergence* of digital technologies, set in a legal environment that is less than transparent.

Fifth, given the complexity of the computing and networking environment and the increase in the number of users, the demand for user support has multiplied manyfold. On the Bloomington campus of IU, the IT organization provides dedicated support to more primary support personnel employed by departments, centers, and schools than it provided to the total number of users just fifteen years ago.

Sixth, fierce competition exists for highly qualified IT professionals; as a result there is unremitting pressure to raise IT salaries. At IU competition for excellent employees comes not only from the private sector and other universities but from departments and schools within the university as they too seek to recruit employees from the central IT organization.

Finally, both users and the wider society are demanding that organizations demonstrate the value that IT adds to the enterprise. In the case of higher education this demand comes first from the users, from faculty, students, and staff who want to be treated as customers. The second, and perhaps more encompassing demand, is phrased in terms of accountability and comes from legislatures, parents, donors, and potential employers, all of whom believe that they are paying the bills and should see value for their money.

In this chapter we outline how one university IT organization, University Information Technology Services (UITS) at Indiana University, has tried to meet these calls for measures of productivity and accountability. We also offer an empirical example of the ongoing results of our efforts. The goal at IU has been to wring the maximum from the resources that UITS has been allotted. We seek to provide an environment in which our colleagues can grow and prosper, to produce IT services of the highest quality, and to add value for the students, faculty, and staff who use these services. In this quest, we have derived measures of quality through systematic surveys of user satisfaction, and we have been able to compute the full costs for each of the services we and our colleagues offer the IU community. The measurement of value has proven a bit more elusive, but we believe it too can be assessed.

Elements of a Solution

Over the last decade there have been massive changes in the culture of IT organizations. Although there are no simple means to describe the successful transformations, there seem to be a few principles and models that can be applied beneficially. The *corporate culture* literature of the 1970s posited several causes of corporate success. First, it was said to be a result of *strong* corporate cultures—no matter how bizarre their manifestations. Then the literature emphasized cultures that nurtured employees. Next came the cultures that focused on profit and performance, the bottom line, and shareholder value. Finally, success was said to be found to be in corporate cultures that embraced a strong commitment to customers and their satisfaction. In fact, as Kotter and Heskett (1992) have demonstrated, none of these cultural foci, in isolation, has been sufficient to achieve success. They showed instead that corporate performance is systematically related to a corporate culture that focuses on customers, employees, and owners in equal measure and contains norms and leadership that promote both adherence to core values and adaptive change in response to changing environments.

Evidence for the importance of diverse models and measures of corporate culture, organization, and performance have come from at least two quarters. First, a pragmatic, anthropological examination of corporate culture reveals that culture, organization, and strategy are all facets of the same phenomenon. As strategy changes, so does an organization and its culture: the one carries out the strategy; the other supports it (see Bate, 1994). It does little good to talk about corporate culture without reference to the goals and strategy of the organization and the structure of the organization itself.

The second approach, the *balanced scorecard,* embraces a disciplined set of diverse measures of organizational performance. This approach "measures organizational performance across four balanced perspectives: financial, customers, internal business processes, and learning and growth" (Kaplan and Norton, 1996, p. 2). The *financial* perspective might include such measures as return on equity (net revenue in terms of invested capital) or economic value added (net revenue minus the cost of capital employed); more and more it is likely to include measures for activity-based costing. The *customers* perspective includes measures of both customer satisfaction and customer perception of quality. In effect this family of dimensions rates products and services according to their "fitness for use" and "freedom from defect," the characteristics that constitute Joseph Juran's (Juran and Gryna, 1988, p. 2.2) primary definition of quality. The evaluation of *internal business processes* might take the form of value chain analysis. This technique measures how value is added at each step, from supplier through production, sale, consumption, after-sale service, and the value actually realized by the customer from the product or service (see especially, Gale, 1994). The analysis of an organization and its culture might also look to process engineering to increase the volume of services, decrease costs, eliminate waste, simplify procedures, and decrease cycle time. *The learning and growth* perspective focuses on measures of staff development, knowledge, and skills. It recognizes that intellectual capital (see Edvinsson and Malone, 1997) is the crucial component in all industries today and that it constitutes the single most important asset of all information technology organizations. Put more starkly, the major assets of a company like Microsoft or an organization like UITS reside in people's heads and leave for home at some point in the day or evening (or leave permanently for a position in another organization).

Robert Kaplan and Robin Cooper (1998) have analyzed the ways that activity-based costing can be applied to the financial and internal business processes of organizations. They show how activity-based costing (ABC) can be used as a foundation for activity-based management (ABM) that supports operational improvements and informs strategic decisions. Operational ABM includes quality and performance management and active cost improvement. Strategic ABM includes everything from improvement in process design through redesign of customer and supplier relationships to the ways markets are segmented and distribution channels are designed.

Shank and Govindarajan (1993) describe a variant of ABC-ABM called strategic cost management (SCM). It too focuses on value chain analysis and the ways linkages with both customers and suppliers can be improved. It admonishes organizations to look constantly for ways that transaction costs can be minimized and production complexity can be stripped out of various processes. It calculates activity costs and includes the cost of poor quality in these activity costs. SCM has shown that for many companies a significant percentage of their customers actually destroy profits and thereby value. That is, poor customer linkage, poor design, and poor quality decrease profits rather than add to them. Finally, SCM looks at strategic positioning, through which products and services can be offered either at low cost (as commodities) or through value and product differentiation (as custom products).

Over the last decade Indiana University's UITS organization and its predecessors have attempted to employ aspects of the models and measures just described. UITS staff have made a conscious effort to examine the structure of the organization and its culture in light of the IT goals set by the faculty and administration. There has been a concerted campaign, backed by resources, to increase the intellectual capital of the organization. The results of customer surveys and calculations of activity costs have been built into process improvement efforts and decisions about process redesign. The internal strategic goals have been focused on continuous improvement and radical redesign of information technology so that UITS might better serve the academic mission of IU. Finally, a sustained effort exists to assess the value of

IT to the academic mission of the university, especially in the area of teaching and learning.

IT Cost, Quality, Culture, and Organization

IT at Indiana University evolved much like IT at other major universities. Administrative and academic computing grew separately until 1988. The two were merged in response to growth in demand for IT services and in the magnitude of investments in the common infrastructure on which both depended. The most important common elements were the inter- and intracampus networks and the growth of the PC as a stand-alone device and as a means to access information resources through a network. Networks and workstations required integrated management and support.

When the academic and administrative computing organizations were merged, their renewed commitment to service was backed by an additional commitment to conduct a statistically valid and professionally administered survey of user satisfaction every year. The survey was opposed initially by several managers, who asserted that users were not competent to judge the quality of the services they were offered and, moreover, that "quality management stuff could only be applied to manufacturing enterprises and not to computer services." Retrospectively, we concluded that the opposition really stemmed from a fear of the unknown customer: at that point very little was known about the ever expanding pool of users, these users' requirements, and the extent to which those requirements were being met. Once these fears were addressed, although not eliminated, the survey was launched. The Indiana University Institute for Survey Research has conducted this survey every year since 1990 (the survey form, numerical evaluations, and users' comments for all these years can be found at www.indiana.edu/~uitssur/survey/index.html).

User surveys over the last decade have provided excellent customer profiles in addition to measures of the quality of IT services. The basic user profile, which includes data from faculty, students, and staff, shows that by 1991, users on the Bloomington campus averaged 14.1 hours of computing service usage per week. By 1998, that usage had grown to an average of 16.7 hours. Faculty, taken as a separate group, used computing services an average of 28.8 hours per week in 1998. Taken all together, users rated the importance of computing services between 4.4 and 4.6 (on a scale of 1 to 5, where 1 is "not at all important" and 5 is "very important") during the years 1991 through 1998. Their average ratings of their own computing skills (on a five-part scale, where 1 equals "novice" and 5 equals "expert") rose from 2.71 in 1991 to 3.19 in 1998.

The decision to institute activity-based costing occurred during a second reorganization. The matrix organization based on functions and technologies that resulted from the merger of academic and administrative computing was unwieldy at best and unproductive at worst. By 1993, it was clear that despite the best efforts of the staff, this organizational structure created too many barriers to effective service delivery. Put bluntly, there were too many conversations that began or ended with "that's not part of my job" or "my group is not responsible for that." At one point the responsibility for electronic mail was fragmented among at least six separate units that were located in every division of the central IT organization. Neither the systems nor the people responsible for supporting them could communicate with one another easily.

Reorganization focused on services that were offered: e-mail and messaging, research computing, Internet, intranets, local area networks, and so forth. Each service, or set of closely related services, and the personnel who created the service or service set were assigned to a strategic service delivery unit (cultural issues precluded calling these units teams). Each service delivery unit was made responsible for its own costs and for the quality of its own services. Figure 3.1 shows a summary representation of a prototypical service and service delivery unit. The cost and quality columns (left and right boxes) define fields for straightforward measures and means of comparison. The center column defines the ways services are produced. That is, it illustrates how talent and skills are combined with business processes, hardware, software, and networks to produce and deliver a service to the IU community. (See the later discussion of student computing facilities for greater process detail.) The elements of ABC are shown on the left side of the figure. Most are straightforward and follow Kaplan and Cooper (1998) and Hope and Hope (1997). The costs for each service comprise the wages and benefits of those who create and deliver the ser-

Figure 3.1. Management Model and Source of Measures for ABC and for Quality Assessment and Improvement

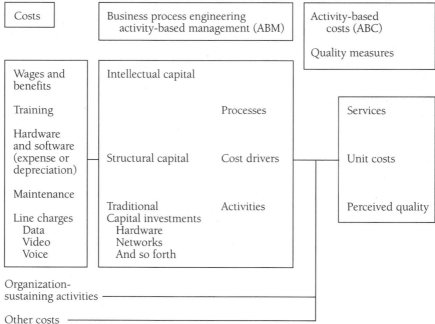

vice; the cost of the hardware, which is generally depreciated over three years; and the cost of the software and maintenance contracts, which are generally treated as expenses. The organization-sustaining activities (at the bottom of the figure) comprise a proportional share of the costs of campus and university IT leadership (vice president's office, dean's office), internal IT management, human resources, security, financial management, and planning functions. The other costs are neither computed directly nor included in the ABC for these services because they are not billed to UITS by the university. These costs include building space, utilities (electricity, heat, air-conditioning, sewage, water, and so forth), and university purchasing office and payroll services.[1]

Value came to the fore in yet a third reorganization. In 1997, the IT organization at the university's Indianapolis campus (IUPUI) was combined with the central IT organization in Bloomington. The combination of these organizations brought experience in the form of a national program for assessment of IT in teaching and learning, the Flashlight Project, to an organization already committed to quality improvement and cost effectiveness. (This project is described in Chapter Four.) IUPUI was a founding member of the Flashlight Project and is currently deploying the project's student survey.

The retrospective value of our quality and cost measurement is detailed in the case study that follows. A discussion of other methods of value assessment forms the conclusion to this chapter.

Case Study: Assessing the Cost and Quality of Student Computing on the Bloomington Campus

Student computing on the Bloomington campus of IU is supported by the student technology fee (STF) and by general fund monies from the academic computing budget. The STF ($5.8 million in fiscal year 1997–98) supported many of the IT services available to approximately thirty-five thousand undergraduate, graduate, and professional students.

In 1997–98, there were 1,105 computers available in thirty-six student technology centers (STCs) on the Bloomington campus, of which 675 (61 percent) are Intel Pentium machines (running on NT 4.0), 374 (34 percent) are Power Macintoshes (running on Mac OS 8.0), and 56 (5 percent) are Unix workstations. Computers in the STCs are connected to servers that manage all the applications offered in these facilities and to other servers that provide each student with 40 MB of on-line storage. All this hardware is on a three-year replacement cycle. For purposes of activity-based costing, the desktop machines, servers, and networking equipment are depreciated over three years, and the residual value (realized through sale to students and faculty) is reflected in the ABC figures.

During 1997–98, 5.8 million seat-hours of computation and 3.1 million seat-hours of consulting were offered in these facilities. During the fall and spring terms more than three thousand hours of instruction were offered in the centers each month.

There are few empty seats at any time of the day or evening in most STCs, and even the least popular locations, well away from the center of student gravity on campus, fill up from time to time. Our tabulations (see Table 3.1) show that the students are connecting to the network and to shared resources, especially mail servers; surfing the Internet; using productivity tools such as word processors and spreadsheets; and using somewhat more specialized applications, such as Photo Shop and Adobe Illustrator, for course assignments in departments like fine arts and geography. The uses of UNIX machines closely parallel NT and Macintosh usage.

Three other IT services are related directly to student use of computers and the network: issuing permanent student network accounts, offering introductory courses in the use of the most common applications and services, and providing each student with up to 40 MB of on-line storage in an FTP server.

Students also consume other information technology services in great quantities. One is access to the network from off campus (never sufficient to the demand); another comprises applications courses offered by UITS in various applications (Sybase, for example), skills (such as those needed to become a Certified Microsoft Engineer), and subjects (such as database management). Students also have access to research computing, high-performance computing, electronic student records, and electronic library catalogues. Perhaps the most popular service for students (aside from e-mail) is the unified student academic and administrative information system (Insite), which allows students to manage their course selections, academic schedules, and financial affairs from a single Web interface. (The costs and perceived quality of these and other services are available on the UITS World Wide Web server, but for the discussion here they are decidedly peripheral.)

Measuring Costs. In the fiscal year 1997–98, the budget for consulting in the STCs was $1.1 million; the budget for hardware, software, maintenance, networking, expendable supplies, and personnel was $3.5 million. In sum, the

Table 3.1. Top Ten Applications for NT and Macintosh Computers in Bloomington Campus STCs, March 1998

NT 4.0 (675 Machines)		Mac OS 8.0 (374 Machines)	
Application	Number of Launches	Application	Number of Launches
McGill Communication	147,489	Telnet (NCSA & better)	78,206
Netscape 4	80,746	Netscape 3 & 2	43,076
MS Word 97	46,847	MS Word 6	14,971
MS Excel	19,266	WordPerfect 3.5	4,837
WordPerfect 8	11,359	Photoshop 4	3,204
Photoshop 4	8,459	FirstClass Client	3,027
Cute FTP	6,625	BB Edit Lite	1,997
MS Access 97	6,150	MS Excel 5	1,936
MS Internet Explorer 3	5,558	Acrobat Reader	1,230
MS PowerPoint 97	4,847	Adobe Illustrator	639

student technology centers consume approximately 60 percent of the student technology fee funds. Account administration receives $172,000 annually, most of which supports the issuance of student accounts; the JumpStart (renamed STEPS in 1998) classes, which are open only to students, receive $230,000 annually; the student portion of the electronic lockers costs approximately $300,000 annually.

The activity-based costs for the core student computing services encompassed by the case study are offered in Table 3.2. It costs approximately $3.00 per student to establish an account, which is done for approximately seven thousand new students every fall; it costs slightly less than $1.00 to support each account. The ninety-minute JumpStart courses in subjects like Microsoft Word and Excel cost $27.15 per student. The cost of 40 MB of on-line storage is $12.00 per user per year.

The costs of services offered in the student technology centers provide far more fertile grounds for analysis and comparison. In fiscal year 1997–98, the full cost of a computer in an STC was $2,436, including the cost of printing from that machine (an average of $252 per machine per year). Thus the average cost of the computer and network attachment exclusive of printing costs is approximately $2,184 per year. The average annual cost of the fifty or so applications provided is $702. So, exclusive of end-user costs, the full cost of each machine including printing is $3,138 per year; the cost without printing is $2,886 per year.

The data in Table 3.2 show the average unit cost of these machines is almost $3,000 less per year than the lowest Gartner Group estimates for minimally configured Wintel machines (Microsoft Windows operating systems

Table 3.2. Activity-Based Costing for STCs

Fiscal Year	1995–96 Actual	1996–97 Actual	1997–98 Actual
Number of student users	35,600	34,700	34,900
Account administration	$2.70/account/year $3.28/action	$0.91/account/year $3.74/action	$0.83/account/year $2.86/action
Number of machines in STCs	938	1,062	1,105
Hardware costs	$2,121/seat $0.47/seat-hour	$2,360/seat $0.44/seat-hour	$2,436/seat $0.47/seat-hour
Software costs	$477/seat $0.10/seat-hour	$831/seat $0.16/seat-hour	$702/seat $0.13/seat-hour
Center consultant costs	$0.31/seat-hour	$0.33/seat-hour	$0.34/seat-hour
On-line storage (40MB)	$18.18/user/year 22,000 users	$11.06/user/year 25,000 users	$12.00/user/year 30,000 users
JumpStart classes	N/A	$35.63/student/class 6,718 students	$27.15/student/class 8,500 students

running on Intel-based machines) or for NetPCs (see Hurwicz, 1998): $2,886 versus $5,500. IU's average cost per machine has remained more or less stable over the last several years, although speed, functionality, and the variety of applications installed on each machine have increased markedly. Furthermore, the cost of software increased from $477 per machine in 1995–96 to $831 in 1996–97 and then decreased to $702 in 1997–98. The jump in cost from 1995 to 1996 and the modest decrease in 1997 can be attributed almost entirely to moving from Windows 3.1 to NT 4.0 on some six hundred Intel machines in 1996 (again, these are full costs, which include the cost of the operating system software and the personnel time and training costs to install and maintain the machines). In summary, the cost to the student (who has paid in advance through the student technology fee) is approximately $1.00 per hour for a fully functional computer, a wide variety of software, and the services of a skilled consultant.

Quality Assessment. The quality of the services offered in the STCs is measured continually through discussions with various advisory groups and annually through the UITS User Survey. Each year for the past decade random samples of Bloomington students, faculty, and staff have been drawn. The student sample size has been one thousand for the last several years. A questionnaire is sent to each student in the sample. The questionnaire asks about the student's use of computers, the student's assessment of his or her own computer expertise, and the student's satisfaction with the services UITS offers. Approximately 43 percent of all those surveyed (student, faculty, and staff) return the questionnaire, a rate that has held steady over the last several years.

The items about the student technology centers and services say UITS "maintains a large number of computer facilities and services specifically designated for student use and instruction. If you use such facilities and services, please indicate your overall satisfaction by circling the appropriate response." (The responses range from 1, "not at all satisfied," through 5, "very satisfied"; they also include the options "never heard of service" and "cannot evaluate.") Table 3.3 presents a summary of student responses on several of the most used services. The numeric score is an unweighted average of the responses from 1 through 5. The percentage satisfied is the proportion who responded with 3 or higher. Account administration—getting and keeping an account—receives consistently good marks. However, 6 percent of the students are dissatisfied with this service. Because UITS distributes seven thousand new accounts every fall during the first week of classes, lines have occasionally been longer than desirable. We believe these lines are the source of most of the dissatisfaction. For the fall of 1998, the process was changed to establish as many accounts as possible during summer orientation. With at least five thousand accounts established in advance of the fall semester, students did not experience the waiting lines that they had in the past. We hope that the 1999 user survey will demonstrate that the change in the way we opened network accounts this fall did make a positive difference in customer satisfaction with this service.

Table 3.3. Selected Quality Measures for Student Computing and for Overall Satisfaction with UITS Service on the Bloomington Campus

Fiscal Year	1995–96		1996–97		1997–98	
	Satisfaction Score	Percentage Satisfied	Satisfaction Score	Percentage Satisfied	Satisfaction Score	Percentage Satisfied
Account administration (all users)	4.06	94.9	4.07	94.4	3.93	93.1
Student technology centers (student evaluations only)						
Hardware	3.96	92.5	3.68	90.2	3.79	93.1
Software	4.2	89.3	3.91	94.2	4.01	96.6
Consultants						
Overall	3.76	89.3	3.73	92	3.66	91.1
Knowledge	N/A	N/A	3.65	87.6	3.71	90.3
Courtesy	N/A	N/A	3.69	87.9	3.78	90.6
On-line storage	3.92	86.6	3.87	89.5	3.70	85.8
JumpStart classes	4.17	94.2	3.89	92.9	3.88	93.8
Overall satisfaction with IT on the Bloomington campus (all users)	3.96	97.5	3.97	95.9	3.92	94.9

The JumpStart classes also get consistently good marks. Here again the expectations and expertise of the entering students increase each year, so courses have to be rewritten and new courses added to meet student needs. This is an excellent example of the Red Queen Hypothesis in action. This group must work very hard just to stay in the same place.

The component services of the student technology centers as rated by the students who use them are generally good. In aggregate these scores are close to very satisfied. They also present some interesting contrasts to one another and through time. The students are generally satisfied with the hardware but wish there were more of it (so say the written comments solicited at the end of the survey form). Last year the satisfaction score for the hardware was 3.8, with 93.1 percent satisfied. Some of the dissatisfaction (about 7 percent) came from reserving STCs for use as classrooms, thereby depriving students of their use as open computing clusters. This policy has now changed, and more STCs have been removed from the potential classroom pool and assigned exclusively for student use. Moreover, UITS is working with the administration to construct computer classrooms designed and scheduled primarily for instruction and supported from general funds rather than the student technology fee.

Student satisfaction with the software in the centers has increased in response to the greater variety offered and to the standardization of applications in the centers with the applications provided to students on IU Ware CDs for use in their residences. This common software permits students to move work in progress easily from home to campus and back home again.

Increase in student satisfaction with the consultants who work in the STCs has been very instructive. At the moment it is pretty good, and it should get even better. When we began in 1988, STC consultants were selected from among self-styled "geeks," "nerds," and "propeller-heads" who applied for employment in order to have access to the Internet and to lots of cool hardware and software. In large measure these consultants were not current students (although many were former students). They possessed knowledge about computers and applications, but in many cases neither their knowledge nor their interests encompassed the machines and software in the particular center to which they were assigned. Moreover, they had little interest in anyone who knew less than they knew about software and hardware—by definition almost everyone they were employed to serve. In 1991, the satisfaction score for these consultants was 3.3, and the percentage satisfied was 76.1 percent. It was clear that something was broken in the way consulting was offered in the STCs.

The method of selecting and training consultants was changed radically in 1994. First, preference is now given to hiring current students. Today 95 percent of the consultants are current, full-time Indiana University students. Second, emphasis is put on part-time positions. Third, training intended to make each consultant an expert in each and every application has been abandoned in favor of general knowledge of how to open, close, and save each application in the three operating systems (NT, MacOS, and UNIX). Furthermore, training is devoted to the use of public and proprietary on-line support systems. Additional training is provided through on-line resources and on-line tutorials developed by UITS. If all these electronic support systems fail, then the ultimate knotty problems can be directed to appropriate UITS specialists for each application and operating system. The end result has been a corps of consultants who are able to use their knowledge and UITS resources to work on any computer platform and answer almost any question presented to them. Fourth, the performance of each consultant is evaluated each term, and continued employment depends upon these evaluations. Finally, the candidate's potential to offer superior customer service is first among the criteria used in the decision to offer employment.

These changes have had both immediate and long-term beneficial consequences. In 1994, the satisfaction score for consultants rose to 3.6, and the percentage satisfied climbed to 86.6 percent. As Table 3.3 shows, the percentage satisfied has been above 90 percent for the last two years. Moreover, a single "how do you rate the consultants?" question has been expanded to ask for a general rating, a knowledge rating, and a courtesy rating. Now fewer than 10 percent of the students who use the STCs are dissatisfied with the services offered by the consultants. The current goal is to convert the majority of that 10 percent to satisfied users.

Balanced Scorecard. Many of the management and organizational themes sketched in the first sections of this chapter are reflected in this small case study. The two strategic service delivery units that offer student technology center services are each responsible for deploying their budgets and for the quality of their services. At most, there is only one individual on the formal organization chart who stands between the managers of these two services and the dean and associate vice president who has responsibility for student computing on the Bloomington campus. The goals for student computing are stated clearly in the campus and university strategic plans for information technology—most recently, *Indiana University Information Technology Strategic Plan: Architecture for the Twenty-First Century* (available at www.indiana.edu/~ovpit/strategic).

The student technology centers provide an illustration of the way culture, strategy, and organization can come together. The central tenet of the UITS culture is that UITS is a service organization and its success depends on the quality of the services it offers; a corollary is that decisions and the responsibility for those decisions are vested in the people who actually do the work and deliver the services. UITS' relatively flat organization allows for creation of new services, change in strategic service delivery units, and movement of individuals between units with a minimum of structural rearrangement and bureaucratic fuss.

The four perspectives of the balanced scorecard, and related models, continue to provide a framework for evaluating and improving the delivery of services in the student technology centers.

The internal business process perspective is represented by clear and explicit written methods for creating and delivering services. Although UITS has no formal process maps, operational procedures and change management guidelines and plans are published, up to date, and available electronically to everyone. There is a clear understanding of just how the assets of the unit are combined to produce the services offered in the STCs.

The learning and growth perspective is addressed in a number of ways. Over the last five years the travel and training budget for the IT organization has been increased 400 percent. These funds are included in the budget of each strategic service delivery unit. Each unit has explicit, written training and professional development goals for each unit member. An employee handbook spells out training requirements. UITS consultants as well as engineers in the STCs are active in EDUCAUSE, and it is not unusual for the consultants to participate in EDUCAUSE meetings and to submit papers. In brief these employees and the intellectual capital they bring to UITS are valued and supported.

The customer perspective of the balanced scorecard has been an integral part of UITS and its culture for almost a decade. The overall satisfaction with UITS and its services has been between 3.9 and 4.0 for the last nine years, and the percentage satisfied has been over 95 percent for most of those years. The one factor that has pulled satisfaction down over the last three years is the lack of sufficient modems and modem lines to meet the demand for service from off campus. Fully one-third of the written comments that are appended to the survey express extreme displeasure at the time it takes to secure a connection during the late afternoon and evening. Given the fixed amount of funds available to support this service, the only way to offer additional access (without making it a charge-back service) is to gain a reduction in the charges levied by the local telephone company for the lines.

Various aspects of the financial perspective of the balanced scorecard are illustrated in the STC example. The ABC data are used both for strategic and operational management of these facilities. One of the strategic issues currently under discussion is just how applications and support will be delivered (and traditional STCs transformed) as laptop computers become the norm (or are required) in various programs and schools. A crucial question will be: How can UITS work with students and prospective students to keep the quality of applications and support services for mobile computing at a high level and also minimize the costs of these services? One way will be to encourage the students to choose laptops with common capabilities, architectures, and applications (without forcing students to select a particular manufacturer or vendor).

Value chain analysis has been invoked explicitly in our insistence on *total life cycle costs* as an element in any purchase agreement with hardware vendors. Such considerations are clearly illustrated also in the university-wide contract negotiated last year with Microsoft for applications and operating systems.

Within the STCs, two very different management methods have been adopted for the provided services. For the Intel-based machines, total life cycle costs, inclusive of support and mean-time-to-failure (cost of poor quality), are the prime considerations. These workstations are managed as commodities, and the supplier has changed at least twice. The Apple Macintosh facilities, which in large measure support graphics applications, likewise are managed from a total cost of ownership perspective, but within the constraints of a single manufacturer. The UNIX facilities are managed for specialized applications and services required by faculty and students in departments like geology, computer science (graphics and visualization), fine arts, and film studies and the School of Public and Environmental Affairs. Life cycle costs are also important here, but both initial and support costs are almost an order of magnitude greater than those of Intel architecture machines.

Value of Information Technology

Although measurements of costs and of perceived quality of information technology services are not easy, both are simple compared to the rigorous assessment of the value of IT in higher education in general and in teaching and learning in specific. The notion that "more IT is better" permeates the business world. This particular mantra—better, perhaps, this particular straw man—has been destroyed on several occasions by Paul Strassmann (most recently, Strassmann, 1997). He points out that the so-called productivity paradox, attributed to MIT economist Michael Solow, is more real than paradoxical. There are too many instances in which increased capital investment in information technology does not lead to a proportional increase in productivity and can, in fact, produce negative economic value added (EVA). (For a sustained criticism of Strassmann's analyses, see National Research Council, 1994, a report that addresses the productivity paradox in service industries; for a more supportive view of Strassmann's work see the U.S. General Accounting Office's *Executive Guide,* 1997.)

T. K. Landauer (1995) offers the most plausible conclusion about the computer paradox. First, he divides computer applications and services into two types: automation and augmentation. Automation encompasses repetitive tasks like statistical analysis, numerical computation, and the production of payroll checks, tasks that if correctly programmed, require little human intervention once they are started. Automation leads to demonstrable gains in productivity and profitability. Augmentation is the use of machines to assist humans in various tasks for which machines cannot be completely substituted for humans and their capabilities. Much of what is on our desktops that goes under the rubrics of decision support, user support, and *knowbots* falls into this second category. Landauer's conclusion is simple: given Juran's definition of quality—fitness for use and freedom from defect—augmentation applications fail miserably on both its counts. They are hard to use and riddled with bugs. Landauer's prescriptions, to which many IT organizations aspire, are rigorous—user-centered design, user-centered development, and user-centered deployment (UCD3).

In the world of higher education the automation component of computation certainly adds value. For example, in this decade the mass of subatomic particles has been evaluated from basic principles of quantum chromodynamics (QCD) by computer (it could not have been calculated otherwise), and the success of this work is among the greatest intellectual achievements of this century. The Human Genome Project relies on clever biochemistry (polymerase chain reaction, or PCR) and massive databases to create a model of human DNA, and a map of the human genome will be available before the turn of the century. The required sorting and matching of snippets of DNA cannot be done other than by computer, at least not on the scale necessary to map the human genome. Vast bodies of published and unpublished works have been digitally encoded and indexed automatically and made available over the network. Each of these examples reduces human transaction costs and completes tasks that are beyond human physical powers but certainly well within the power of the human intellect.

Likewise, on the administrative side of the institution, automation manages most of the repetitive business functions. It functions as a clerk in keeping track of library books and sending out overdue notices; it places students in various sections of English 101 and even keeps track of drop-adds so that students on a wait-list can automatically be given a seat once one becomes free. It keeps the general ledger, keeps track of capital equipment, and produces transcripts on demand. However, when it comes to decision support and other augmentation applications, universities are no better off than firms in the private sector.

The advent of the World Wide Web has placed various augmentation tools, a selection of search engines and intelligent filters, where everyone can pick and choose from them. The Web has been a boon to research and scholarship. Almost every paper and source of information mentioned in the sections that follow is available only from a Web source. Likewise, library catalogues, electronic journals, and scholarly databases are available at the click of a mouse button and can be printed at one's desk with a click of the same button. There are, however, two problems inherent in these electronic sources of information. The first concerns their persistence. Just how long will papers endure when they are published only in electronic form and available only in one place? Second, leaving aside the electronic journals of established associations and libraries, because they have been subject to peer review at many levels, how does one ascertain the veracity and accuracy of sources available via the Internet? The development of an appropriate level of sophisticated critical judgment in students is one of the tasks that faces faculty in all institutions of higher education.

Measuring the value of information technology in teaching and learning is the topic of another question, one that is far from resolution. The assessment of pedagogy in higher education has achieved a degree of urgency and sophistication in the last two decades (for example, Banta and Associates, 1993; Banta, Lund, Black, and Oblander, 1996; Astin, 1992, 1993). However, the role of information technology has not been investigated in the vast majority of the assessments thus far. If there is value to the integration of information technology in higher education—beyond computation and connectivity—it remains to be systematically demonstrated and documented by the assessment community.

We can offer one small, anecdotal set of data that measures the perceived value of information technology on the Bloomington campus. For the last two years questions about value have been included in the UITS User Survey (using a scale of 1, "not at all helpful," to 5, "very helpful"). Faculty have been asked: "How helpful has the computing and network environment at IU been in your teaching activities?" In 1997, 73 percent of the faculty said they used information technology in their teaching, and they rated its helpfulness at 3.72; in 1998, 86.1 percent said they used information technology, and they rated it at 3.78. Students have been asked: "How helpful has the computing and network environment been in your learning experience at IU?" In 1997, 97.4 percent of undergraduate and graduate students said that they used information technology in their classes, and they rated its helpfulness at 4.15; in 1998, 98.3 percent acknowledged use of information technology in their classes, and they rated it at 4.14.

In brief, the value of information technology in the syllabus and in the classroom has neither been rigorously measured nor comprehensively studied. At best universities are left with the classic vetting lines, "nothing known against" and "no significant difference" (Russell, 1996). Demonstration of value will require synchronic and diachronic samples of students, classes, and the use of information technology that currently seem beyond the means and commitments of most institutions.

The quests for measures of cost and quality and for measurement of value in the operation of institutions of higher education are scattered among scholars and institutions throughout North America and Europe. What we report here is not unique either to Indiana University or to UITS. The pursuit of quality has been reported for both curricular and business operations of higher education in the United States (Seymour 1993, 1995; Roberts 1995). The National Science Foundation, the Motorola Corporation, and IBM, among others, support quality improvement plans and research in universities. UITS' use of activity-based costing and strategic cost management fits with the use of responsibility center budgeting and management, which was adopted by Indiana University in 1988 (Whalen, 1991). UITS can offer intelligent support for the assessment of information technology in teaching and learning, but leadership in this quest is rightly vested in the faculty, the academic deans, and the provost (at IU, the dean of the faculties). The real value of these families of measures is in how they frame ongoing discussions about budgets, performance, and results. UITS and its budget are part of a university that values, along with aesthetics and ethics, argument and evidence above all else (although aesthetics and ethics have coequal status). Universities and their cultures ask that in any argument about facts, the argument is rational and the evidence is reliable and replicable. Measures of quality, ABC measures and benchmarks, and demonstrations of value are the critical elements in all such discussions.

Note

1. To compare the costs for UITS services with external, private sector benchmarks, add 13 percent to the Web-published ABC for the service (10 percent for space and utilities; 3 percent for other university services). The complete activity-based costing for the last three fiscal years, 1995–96 through 1997–98, and an authoritative description of each service can be found on the Web (www.indiana.edu/~uits/business/indexbl.html).

References

Astin, A. W. *What Matters in College? Four Critical Years Revisited.* San Francisco: Jossey-Bass, 1992.

Astin, A. W. *Assessment for Excellence: The Philosophy and Practice of Assessment and Evaluation in Higher Education.* Phoenix, Ariz.: Oryx Press, 1993.

Banta, T. W., and Associates. *Making a Difference: Outcomes of a Decade of Assessment in Higher Education.* San Francisco: Jossey-Bass, 1993.

Banta, T. W., Lund, J. P., Black, K. E., and Oblander, F. W. *Assessment in Practice: Putting Principles to Work on College Campuses.* San Francisco: Jossey-Bass, 1996.

Bate, P. *Strategies for Cultural Change.* Portsmouth, N.H.: Butterworth-Heinemann, 1994.

Carroll, L. *Alice in Wonderland.* (D. J. Gray, ed.) New York: Norton, 1992. (Originally published 1897.)

Edvinsson, L., and Malone, M. S. *Intellectual Capital.* New York: Harper Business, 1997.

Gale, B. T. *Managing Customer Value.* New York: Free Press, 1994.

Hope, J., and Hope, T. *Competing in the Third Wave: The Ten Key Management Issues of the Information Age.* Boston: Harvard Business School Press, 1997.

Hurwicz, M. "Managing PC Costs." *Byte,* 1998, 23 (7), 65–71.

Juran, J. M., and Gryna, F. M. (eds.). *Juran's Quality Control Handbook.* (4th ed.) New York: McGraw-Hill, 1988.

Kaplan, R. S., and Cooper, R. *Cost and Effect: Using Integrated Cost Systems to Drive Profitability and Performance.* Boston: Harvard Business School Press, 1998.

Kaplan, R. S., and Norton, D. P. *The Balanced Scorecard.* Boston: Harvard Business School Press, 1996.

Kotter, J. P., and Heskett, J. L. *Corporate Culture and Performance.* New York: Free Press, 1992.

Landauer, T. K. *The Trouble with Computers: Usefulness, Usability, and Productivity.* Cambridge, Mass.: MIT Press, 1995.

National Research Council. *Information Technology in the Service Society: A Twenty-First Century Lever.* Washington, D.C.: National Academy Press, 1994.

Roberts, H. V. (ed.). *Academic Initiatives in Total Quality for Higher Education.* Milwaukee, Wisc.: ASQC Quality Press, 1995.

Russell, T. "The No Significant Difference Phenomenon." Bibliography of research results on the impact of various technologies and correspondence study on teaching and learning, 1928 to 1996. [www.teleeducation.nb.ca/nosignificantdifference].

Seymour, D. *On Q: Causing Quality in Higher Education.* Phoenix, Ariz.: Oryx Press, 1993.

Seymour, D. *Once upon a Campus: Lessons for Improving Quality and Productivity in Higher Education.* Phoenix, Ariz.: Oryx Press, 1995.

Shank, J. K., and Govindarajan, V. *Strategic Cost Management: The New Tool for Competitive Advantage.* New York: Free Press, 1993.

Strassmann, P. A. *The Squandered Computer: Evaluating the Business Alignment of Information Technologies.* New Canaan, Conn.: Information Economics Press, 1997.

U.S. General Accounting Office. *Executive Guide: Measuring Performance and Demonstrating Results of Information Technology Investments.* GAO/AIMD-97-163. Washington, D.C.: U.S. General Accounting Office, 1997.

Whalen, E. L. *Responsibility Centered Budgeting: An Approach to Decentralized Management for Institutions of Higher Education.* Bloomington: Indiana University Press, 1991.

CHRISTOPHER SPALDING PEEBLES *is professor of anthropology, director of the Glenn A. Black Laboratory of Archaeology, associate vice president for research and academic computing, and dean for information technology at Indiana University.*

LAURIE G. ANTOLOVIC *is chief financial officer of the Office of the Vice President for Information Technology at Indiana University.*

NORMA B. HOLLAND *is the associate vice president for university information systems at Indiana University.*

KAREN HOEVE ADAMS *is executive officer in the Indiana University Office of the Vice President for Information Technology.*

DEBBY ALLMAYER *is human resources officer for the Office of the Vice President for Information Technology at Indiana University.*

PHYLLIS H. DAVIDSON *is director of information technology for Indiana University libraries.*

As the largest university in its state, Virginia Polytechnic Institute and State University (Virginia Tech) has developed a reputation as a computer-intensive, technology-rich environment. This chapter describes the growth of this environment, the evolving relationship between technology and teaching and learning, and how assessment has recently assumed an integral role in that relationship's development.

Assessing the Changing Impact of Technology on Teaching and Learning at Virginia Tech: A Case Study

C. David Taylor, Joanne D. Eustis

In recent years the U.S. system of higher education has suffered from an erosion of confidence among the public, who seem to believe that the values and preferences of research universities in particular have become disconnected from the ethics and needs of society at large (Sykes, 1990). This disconnection has manifested itself in questions about the quality and relevance of undergraduate education and in demands from governing boards and funding agencies for more accountability and productivity. Universities have been charged with failing to prepare students to live and work in a global world, engaging in studies that are out of harmony with contemporary society, and failing to involve students in a dynamic, relevant learning process.

In response defenders of higher education argue that new information technologies offer means to remedy the situation and accommodate the learning needs of an expanding and increasingly diverse student population. To this end higher education has indeed been aggressive in adopting state-of-the-art technologies but slow in adjusting its organizational structure and processes to leverage these technologies' potential. In the words of Vartan Gregorian, former president of Brown University, "the new technology per se is not a revolution—the revolution is the difference that technology makes in how we organize, structure, and empower our lives" (Gregorian, Hawkins, and Taylor, 1992, p. 7). In recognition of the power and potential of technology, the State Council of Higher Education for Virginia (SCHEV) has mandated that the use of technology become an integral part of higher education's restructuring efforts. The message from SCHEV is clearly stated in a list of suggested restructuring objectives and actions (State Council of Higher Education for Virginia, 1995), among which are the following:

- Improve quality and reduce costs of instruction
- Incorporate technology
- Increase faculty productivity
- Serve students at new sites
- Offer credit for competency and self-paced learning

However, the importance of technology in the teaching-learning process is not a new concept in the state. During the 1988 session of Virginia's General Assembly, then-governor Gerald Baliles charged the Virginia Commission on the University of the Twenty-First Century (1990) "to develop a vision of higher education to meet the demands of the next century." A report written at Virginia Tech by the University Task Force on the Impact of Digital Technology on the Classroom Environment (1989) played a prominent role in the commission's discussion of technology. The commission report stated that in the university of the twenty-first century, "the constraints of space and time will be reduced by thoughtful introduction of telecommunications and computers into the instructional mission of colleges and universities." The commission further stated:

> New digital technology offers the promise of three significant changes in faculty-student contact:
>
> 1. The nature of formally structured contact will shift.
> 2. A larger part of faculty/student contact will be ad hoc and relatively unstructured.
> 3. The provision of an electronic message system will allow extensive contact without requiring student and teacher to be in the same place" [p. 7].

Viewed with hindsight this list of predictions appears remarkably prescient. Virginia's legislature has included the use of technology as "an area of emphasis" in the restructuring of the commonwealth's institutions of higher education.

Uses of Technology in Higher Education

For almost a century institutions of higher education made few changes in the way they delivered instructional services. For the most part teaching has been *synchronous,* meaning that students and faculty members meet physically in the same place at the same time. The predominant instructional model has been lecture and test. Calls for reform insist that the focus must shift from this passive receptor model to an independent learning model, with an emphasis on students' more active engagement in the learning process. To this end technologies have been combined to create gateways for scholars and students to vast sources of information in various forms: voice, video and images, text, interactive databases. These gateways—the most prevalent being the World Wide Web, or Internet—provide unparalleled opportunities for asynchronous, *on-demand* learning through access to a remote resource at the student's convenience. Advocates claim tremendous benefits for asynchronous learning, including greater opportunities for collaborative learning among students, greater interaction, and increases in individual productivity (Taylor, Roy, and Moore, 1997).

This new learning paradigm compellingly advocates a departure from what Carol Twigg (1994) calls "faculty-centered curricula," in which faculty habits and interests take precedence over student-centered learning. Twigg asserts that in college and university courses, "design all too frequently begins with the question, 'What do I want to teach?' rather than 'What do the students need to learn?'" She writes: "The concept of course design itself is indicative of a faculty-centered approach: faculty design, faculty select, faculty present. In the process, the student is often little more than a passive recipient of the outcomes of the faculty member's decision-making process" (p. 18).

Herein lies a challenge. When institutions of higher education use technology, the decision regarding what and how students learn should be the result of collaborative decision making by faculty members, instructional design specialists, learning assessment experts, students, and college and university administrators working within the context of the demands for institutional change. Yet such a radical cultural shift cannot come easily or without questions about the nature and effects of the changes. How does an academic institution make decisions about new directions in course content and modes of learning given its shared governance system and a community with diverse values and agendas? Virginia Tech serves well as a case in point, because it is both typical and atypical in its history of using technology in advancing learning.

Most institutions in the corporate and government sector as well as in higher education relied heavily on centralized mainframes and minicomputers throughout the 1970s and 1980s. Personal computers were not taken seriously until their computing power began to rival that of older mainframes, and they did not begin to supercede the centralized mainframe systems until networking and communication technology became an affordable reality in the early 1990s. Although computers have been used for instructional purposes since the late 1960s and on an increasing scale at Virginia Tech since the late 1980s and early 1990s, these early instructional applications were mostly isolated ventures, restricted in their impact to a single course or part of a course. However, two initiatives at Virginia Tech are worth mentioning because of their departure from this pattern.

First, in 1984, the College of Engineering, under the leadership of Dean Paul Torgersen (now president of Virginia Tech), instituted a requirement that each student have his or her own personal computer and a set of associated engineering software tools. This was the first college of engineering in the nation to institute such a requirement. Each year, as the technology has become more advanced, specifications for the student-purchased PCs are upgraded in order to ensure that engineering students experience and experiment with the leading edge of technology. This is one of the few examples of a technological initiative so widely adopted that it affected every member of a large population.

Second, Virginia Tech was a key participant in the SUCCEED project, again through the College of Engineering. Initially funded by the National Science Foundation in 1992, the Southeastern University and College Coalition for Engineering Education (SUCCEED) is a group of southeastern universities' engineering colleges that make use of new technologies to improve teaching, especially the teaching of highly theoretical courses that traditionally have been difficult for students. The member institutions each contribute a variety of developments to the project. For example, Virginia Tech created and hosted a database of engineering-related images that any faculty member could download for educational use across the then-fledgling Internet. This project was important because it not only had an impact within Virginia Tech but also enabled a cooperative sharing of curricula and ideas among several institutions. One of SUCCEED's major objectives is to improve the engineering curriculum using outcomes assessment results, and one of the "products" produced as a result of Virginia Tech's first five-year SUCCEED grant was a learning objectives and outcomes assessment planning guide for engineering academic administrators [see www.succeed.vt.edu].

Investment in Teaching and Learning

The decade of the 1990s has seen a continuation of Virginia Tech's innovation and steady progress toward the incorporation of technology into teaching and learning methodologies and communications. A number of programs—the Instructional Development Initiative, Cyberschool and the ACCESS project, and the Center for Innovation in Learning—have been initiated, accompanied by an increasing interest in a role for assessment.

Instructional Development Initiative. Virginia Tech Instructional Services (a unit formerly called the Learning Resources Center and then Media Services) has existed since the early 1970s. The Center for Excellence in Undergraduate Teaching (CEUT) was established in 1993 to foster instructional excellence and innovation. Despite these resources and innumerable directives from SCHEV, there was little evidence until recently of interest among faculty members in teaching methodologies that used technologies. For example, SCHEV provided funds in 1992 for a Virginia Tech faculty grants program that allowed Educational Technologies (a department within Instructional Services) to gain valuable experience in managing three technology-based course transformation projects. However, these projects affected only individual courses and had minimal impact outside their home departments.

There was of course a pragmatic reason contributing to the indifference to technological innovation. At Virginia Tech operating budgets had been flat or declining for a decade, and such constrictions naturally limit the discretionary spending of academic administrators. In departments without significant sources of outside income, there had been a particularly acute lack of funds for traditional support, let alone for new equipment. As a result, managerial initiative was thwarted, and only limited discretionary choices remained, except at the highest level of the university administration. Consequently, local experimentation with pedagogical innovation and the development of alternative teaching strategies, especially those using technology, did not enjoy wide appeal or encouragement.

During the early 1990s, Virginia Tech was typical of many universities in undergoing severe budget cuts amid an atmosphere of public hostility toward higher education in general and faculty in particular (see, for example, Walzer, 1993). Not surprisingly, faculty morale had sunk to an all-time low. At this point the vice president for information systems and the university provost made a courageous and far-reaching decision: rather than continue to retrench and cut back, they decided to redirect resources and invest in the faculty, students, and the teaching infrastructure, using technology as a vehicle. Therefore, in 1993, the Instructional Development Initiative (IDI), developed jointly by Information Systems and the Office of the Provost, was proposed and subsequently funded centrally. The goals of the program were outlined in the document *Phase II: Instructional Development Initiative,* for the 1994–98 fiscal period, and were organized into the following three components:

Faculty Development Initiative (FDI)

- Provide the opportunity for all faculty in the University to participate in this faculty development program. The overarching goal is to motivate them to investigate, create, and utilize alternative instructional strategies.
- Provide participants who complete the program with access to state-of-the-art instructional technology, the knowledge to use it, and the motivation to collaborate with their colleagues in leveraging instructional technology in their courses.

Student Access

- Provide advice to all students on their investment in computer technology in order to maximize its usefulness during their college careers.
- Provide better access to computing resources for all students who do not have their own personal computers and provide computer labs for accessing specialized software which is unique to disciplinary areas (such as Perseus, Mathematica, and Daedalus).
- Provide network-based training materials for students in order to ensure that they have a basic foundation in the use of computing and instructional technology resources.

Course Development

- Support faculty in the development of network accessible courseware and instruction.
- Facilitate the development of electronic libraries of scholarly materials supporting designated courses.
- Provide improved classroom and presentation facilities to support faculty efforts in introducing new technologies into core curriculum courses [Virginia Polytechnic Institute and State University, 1995, p. 15].

An additional, unstated goal was to enable the transformation of the university's computing infrastructure from a mainframe to a client-server architecture.

In fiscal year 1993–94, as the FDI began its first series of workshops but even before it began to have a campuswide influence, a number of concurrent technology-related developments were occurring as a result of the robust technology climate at Virginia Tech. One unique project was the Blacksburg Electronic Village (BEV) (see www.bev.net). BEV was developed as the result of a desire to extend Virginia Tech's network access beyond campus boundaries. For any computer network to be used to its potential for instructional purposes, students living off campus required access to network-based information services. Therefore in 1991, a decision was made to offer, in collaboration with the town of Blacksburg and Bell Atlantic, Internet access to the local community. After two years of infrastructure development the first distribution of BEV software was tested in 1993. The subsequent rapid growth of BEV was a harbinger of the future national development of the Internet and the incredible proliferation of Internet service providers (ISPs) and Web sites around the world, and led to a spate of newspaper and magazine articles, such as one in *USA Today* that called Blacksburg "the most-wired town in America."

Cyberschool and the ACCESS Project. In November of 1994, a group of arts and sciences faculty—all of whom had participated in the first FDI—proposed that more valuable than getting "computers into the classroom" would be "getting classrooms out of computers." This loosely organized, multidisciplinary group of faculty members has proceeded to test the efficacy and push the limits of computer-mediated communication technologies. What these faculty have discovered is described in a number of position papers that may be found on the Cyberschool Web site (www.cyber. vt.edu/docs/papers.html; see also, more generally, www.cyber.vt.edu/ default.html). They have been a constant source of innovation, inspiration, and discovery regarding the strengths and limitations of learning networks. Cyberschool today functions as a forum for information interchange, as a support group for faculty pioneers, and as a creative voice for advocating policy changes to the administration. It remains a valuable channel of communication between early adopters of technology and the majority of faculty and administrators.

As an ad hoc group of faculty, Cyberschool was largely an unfunded entity and remains so today. In order to develop many of the ideas originating in Cyberschool in a substantive and programmatic way, Associate Dean Lucinda Roy, one of Cyberschool's cofounders, initiated a request to the Alfred P. Sloan Foundation for funding to explore the concept of asynchronous learning networks (ALN). The College of Arts and Sciences, Educational Technologies (as part of Instructional Services), and three faculty from the department of biology were subsequently funded to transform four lower-division, introductory biology courses in a project called ACCESS (Asynchronous Communications Courses to Ensure Student Success).

Biology courses were chosen for several reasons. First, the three faculty were not only willing to participate but also had the drive and experience to have introduced creative and far-reaching technological and instructional innovation into their own courses. Second, there was a deep need for change in the department, because it was faced with an unprecedented influx of new students. Finally, biology had, more than most departments, settled on the large lecture model for its lower-division courses, and faculty and administration alike had recently realized that simply continuing to increase the size of classes was no longer a viable option. With growing class sizes, few resources for teaching support, and a student population that was ever more technologically sophisticated and demanding, the large lower-division biology lecture courses were prime candidates for transformation.

ACCESS was funded in December of 1995. Development, implementation, and assessment proceeded for eighteen months and concluded in the summer of 1997. Some ACCESS developments included a widely emulated course Web site that provided round-the-clock access to class materials (lecture slides, notes, the syllabus), class news and announcements, links to outside resources, and a communication forum. The more important innovations included experimentation with a variety of new communication channels among students and between students and faculty, which extended class discussions far beyond the confines of the classroom. The complete results are available in the final report, which was published on-line in the summer of 1997 (see www.edtech.vt.edu/access).

From the point of view of this chapter, one particularly important project innovation was the emphasis placed on evaluation and assessment. The Sloan Foundation requested that assessment be a major part of the project and increased the size of the grant in order to fund that part of the initiative. The assessment effort attempted to answer questions related to asynchronous communication and new teaching and learning models; the use of technology to relieve faculty of repetitive tasks; self-paced learning in large, mixed ability classes; the efficient development of course materials; the impact of technology on learning, motivation, and student success; and the identification of essential faculty and student skills for the new age of learning. These were ambitious goals for any assessment effort, but the lessons learned during ACCESS informed an approach to assessment that was used in the much larger technology projects that were to come.

Center for Innovation in Learning. Recently (1996–98), the grassroots technology activity of faculty has increased across campus, spurred on by a heightened level of awareness of the possibilities of the new technologies. Participants in the Faculty Development Initiative workshops have begun to request more help in using technologies in their courses. In addition, the administration has encouraged development of distance learning courses, and deans and department heads have begun to identify those courses that could benefit from the use of technology. In order to aid development, the Center for Innovation in Learning (CIL) was founded in 1996 to integrate research on teaching and learning into the curriculum. CIL's work is based on the assumption that instructional innovation is accomplished through the interaction of design, development, delivery, and marketing. Through faculty projects, the center investigates, develops, researches, tests, and evaluates new technology-based teaching and learning approaches, particularly those related to distance learning, faculty development, instructional technologies, and telecommunications. A third round of annual grant awards was completed in the spring of 1998, and to date sixty-six projects have been funded for over $1.5 million.

The technological and pedagogical changes required to develop distance learning courses and campus Web-based courses overlap to a great extent, and spurred on by CIL funding, the pace of course transformation in both these areas has rapidly increased. Simultaneously, a massive upgrade in the state network infrastructure has created an opportunity for a quantum increase in distance learning course distribution. Information Systems has laid the groundwork for the development of NET.WORK.VIRGINIA, a state-of-the-art, wide area educational network. This advanced broadband network will deliver ATM (asynchronous transfer mode) service statewide and already connects 120 participating sites, including all four-year colleges and universities, the Virginia Community College System, several K–12 school systems, and many state agencies.

Marketing is essential to the promulgation and acceptance of any new initiative, and Virginia Tech Online (VTOnline) was established by the CIL in 1997 as a mechanism for communication among and coordination of net-centered activities. As a central Web site (www.vto.vt.edu), VTOnline serves as a single point of contact for all computer-mediated instructional and information services across the university. It provides easy-to-use information about all instructional, administrative, and public service activity that is available at Virginia Tech over the Internet. It acts as an organizing point within the university that coordinates information concerning on-line degree programs, short courses, extension activities, and support for public service initiatives for the continual development of all existing and new network-centered teaching initiatives, ranging from course and program innovation to assessment and evaluation practices.

Evolution of a Strategy for Assessing Instructional Technologies

As a result of the overwhelming increase in activity requiring technological support, there has been a groundswell of interest in and demand for assessment of technology projects and their impact on the university's most fundamental mission—teaching and learning. Furthermore, as resources have been diverted from other activities into instructional technology projects, new computing and network infrastructure, and course redesign, questions of impact, of costs versus benefits, and of efficiency have naturally arisen. In addition, an awareness of new roles for faculty has begun to permeate the university culture. For example, the idea that faculty need both released time and considerable support (expert assistance, training, consulting, additional hardware and software) in order to revise and transform their courses has evolved from a novel luxury to an accepted expectation.

Yet as time goes by it seems that more questions are raised than answered. Faculty developers ask: How can my courses be improved? Which technology is most appropriate, or more fundamentally, is technology necessary for this improvement? What kind of and how much assistance will I need—how many people or machines or resources will be required? When I start implementing changes to the course, how will the students react, what will their expectations be? These are not questions that faculty are typically experienced in answering or that they expected to confront when they began their academic careers by lecturing, doing research, and serving on committees. Administrators and department heads have a different set of questions. Once the decision to support course transformation is made, they ask: How will we allocate resources, and whom will we support? How will we manage the changes being proposed? How will development activities affect the traditional areas of faculty productivity? How will we monitor the student reaction to these changes? Eventually everyone involved must at some time present a coherent picture of the project and its outcomes to other faculty, upper administration, the board of regents, professional conferences, governmental agencies, legislators, and parents. A good assessment plan can help address most of these questions, and it can certainly aid in communicating results to interested outsiders.

CNI Project: A Unified Approach to Assessment. In a call for statements of interest and experience, the Coalition for Networked Information (CNI) invited institutions of higher education, in December 1996, "to use ongoing assessment techniques to study the uses, impacts, costs, and effectiveness of networks and networked resources and services." One of nine institutions chosen to participate in CNI's Assessing the Academic Networked Environment project, Virginia Tech formed an interdisciplinary team that included representation from the library, computing center, instructional services, and network services. Work proceeded on assessment of various aspects of network activities and services throughout 1997.

A great deal of uncoordinated and overlapping assessment activity was discovered within Virginia Tech Information Systems. Although committed—and indeed, required—to measure the effectiveness of network use and instructional technology, the people responsible for network infrastructure development, maintenance of communications systems, and the delivery of network-based information services, support, and instruction were not necessarily communicating among themselves. A great benefit of participation in the project was the opportunity to network, share, and coordinate the results of individual assessment efforts. Equally important, it increased understanding of the interdependence in a networked environment.

Purpose of Assessment. As developers and administrators at Virginia Tech, our experience with assessment grew largely out of the ACCESS project, was modified by the group experience with the CNI affiliation, and has continued to evolve with the ongoing assessment of the much larger CIL initiative. The goals for assessment are therefore practical and needs driven. First and foremost, assessment must be *useful*. It should not involve collecting data for their own sake. Although it uses many of the methods of basic research, assessment is research with an end in mind; in traditional terms, it is applied research.

The two purposes of assessment can best be summarized as *feedback* and *communication*. The feedback function (also known as formative evaluation) serves the purpose of informing persons directly involved with the project or intervention about its progress. The central idea is that given timely and useful information, a midcourse correction might be made that could increase the effectiveness and chances of success of the project. To be useful in a rapidly evolving project, feedback data must be quickly collected and analyzed but by necessity this analysis will be somewhat less rigorous than the final or summative evaluation upon which the final judgment about project outcomes might be made.

Communication is the ultimate rationale for the assessment of projects or interventions. Practically speaking, if results are not communicated to the outside world, then except for the benefits to the immediate participants, the project might as well not have been undertaken in the first place. Above all, did the project meet its goals? For example, increased learning may or may not be a goal, but if it is, how did learning occur, and how was it measured? In any case, what were the outcomes? What are the different parts or aspects of the project, and which were successful? What was the impact? Who was affected by the project and to what extent? Can the project's innovations be transferred or scaled up to more students, to other programs? Can these innovations reduce costs? Are these findings useful in determining whether the project should be continued or expanded? If so, how could it be improved? Moreover, different audiences need different kinds of information. The participants and immediate stakeholders—at Virginia Tech the faculty developers, staff, students, and administrators who form the development and implementation team—will first want the kind of practical, formative evaluation and feedback described in the previous paragraph. Outsiders, however, will be interested in the long-range, summative outcomes of the project. They either want to apply the findings to their own situations, or they are decision makers who want to know where and how to allocate future resources.

Methodologies. Assessment methods at Virginia Tech are in a constant state of evolution, but in general the emphasis is on a holistic description of the intervention—a snapshot of the status of the project. To achieve this holistic picture, quantitative and qualitative data are combined in a hybrid design and findings are reported in a narrative, descriptive format within which data are embedded as evidence. Most important is the framework for the assessment activities, that is, the questions that need to be answered or the criteria for success of the project or intervention. It is crucial that this framework be reviewed, negotiated, and agreed upon well in advance by all stakeholders. Assessment data include traditional numerical or quantitative measurements (census data, survey results, grades), but they also include a large portion of qualitative data such as material from interviews and observations and also summaries and quotes from various textual sources. The two types of data complement each other but are considerably different and are therefore discussed separately in the following sections.

Qualitative Methods and Data. In *Assessing the Academic Networked Environment: Strategies and Options,* Charles McClure and Cynthia Lopata (1996) give a succinct definition of qualitative data: "Qualitative data are data that describe, explain, and characterize the subject of investigation using words rather than numbers." They go on to note that qualitative methods are appropriate "where the research problem and the research setting are *not* well understood" (p. 11). Most course transformations that involve instructional technologies fit this situation. Although faculty and other developers will have certain objectives for their projects, they cannot pretend to know everything that will happen when changes are implemented. Furthermore, they fully expect to make changes along the way. Given this state of change and uncertainty, the usual data-gathering tool, the survey, with its specific questions and limited response criteria, could easily fail to capture major effects. The solution is to use qualitative, ethnographic research methods; that is, talk to the participants and observe them in a natural setting, and above all be good listeners and good observers and be open to the unexpected and the obvious. In this way the participants themselves can raise issues that the planners and evaluators did not anticipate.

Qualitative methods are ideal for finding out, from a holistic point of view, the impact of new technologies or instructional interventions. In addition to observing classes, labs, and other class activities such as field trips, our primary instrument for gathering data was the guided interview (Patton, 1990), in which the interviewer follows a list of questions but also feels free to depart from that script and explore topics that the subject initiates or in which the subject seems to have interest or knowledge. Other methods we have employed include focus groups, benchmarking, and examination of user activities, through transcripts of on-line discussions, for example. A complete description of qualitative research methods along with a rationale for their use is obviously beyond the scope of this chapter, and the reader is referred to comprehensive works on the subject (Patton, 1990; Denzin and Lincoln, 1994; Miles and Huberman, 1994). Finally, the findings of open-ended interviews help inform the writing of subsequent surveys and point the direction in which to look with more precise and widely accepted quantitative methods.

The primary practical problem in qualitative methods is accumulating more data than can comfortably be organized, analyzed, and interpreted. Open-ended interviews can be lengthy and must be transcribed, checked for accuracy, then coded and studied. The results must be organized, analyzed, summarized, and *displayed,* or presented. In addition, field observation is time consuming and requires a disciplined researcher to observe, take useful notes or record observations, and then compile the notes into a useful format. Finally, almost any textual material is grist for the qualitative mill, and technology interventions leave an extensive textual trail suitable for analysis: on-line discussions, e-mail interchanges, listservs, threaded discussion groups—all are raw material that can be archived and incorporated into the data set.

For all their difficulties, we have found that qualitative data have a great deal of value and impact in communicating the nature of a project, which was the bottom line of our assessment effort. When embedded in a readable narrative, qualitative data such as quotes from student or faculty interviews make immediate sense and are accessible to everyone, which is often not the case for a complex statistical analysis. We have also found that technology allows the impact and credibility of qualitative data to be extended beyond the normal paper-based report. In the ACCESS project, we videotaped as many of the interviews with students and faculty as possible, which was quite acceptable to almost all of the interview subjects. Because the videotaping and sound recording was done at a high level of quality, clips from these interviews could then be used in a wide variety of applications: as part of traditional videotapes, on CD-ROMs, or as part of multimedia presentations. For example, we included approximately forty of these clips in the on-line version of the ACCESS report (see www.edtech.vt.edu/access). Although the right quote has tremendous impact in a text narrative, it is even more powerful to see and hear the student or professor actually saying those same words.

Quantitative Methods and Data. Our standard method of data collection was the survey, administered to an intact class. Typically, we tried to find out as much as possible about the students' background and their use of computers and networks, including demographics, computer ownership, knowledge of and experience with computer networks, and attitudes toward different ways of learning (cooperative groups, independent study, relative importance of lecture versus lab, and so forth). We also administered a computer attitude scale (Ray and Minch, 1990), usually at the beginning and end of the semester, which gave us an indication of students' anxieties about and alienation from computer technology and how these feelings changed during the course of the semester. Finally, we asked many specific questions about technology in the class: their usage of the class Web site, the impact of the class and technology on their attitudes toward the course subject matter, their opinion on the usefulness of the technology, and so forth.

Most of our analyses used descriptive data as a way of summarizing responses. We were also able to use the data, however, for some interesting correlation studies and tests of significance. For example, many faculty were concerned that students who owned computers or were more favorably disposed toward or adept with computer and network technology might have an unfair advantage in a technology-enhanced class. We were able to report that, to date, there has been no significant correlation between computer ownership, experience, or attitude (that is, computer anxiety and alienation) and course grades. We also found that computer attitude scores in many technology-enhanced courses improved significantly between the beginning and end of the semester.

Flashlight Project: A National Link. As useful as these survey data were, we continued to have doubts that we were asking the right questions regarding the important questions that were repeatedly asked in conversations, in meetings, and at conferences: Did students learn more as a result of using the technology? Are these technologies cost efficient and better than courses without technology? Fortunately, the Flashlight Project (see www.tltgroup.org) has provided a useful approach and a tool for answering these questions. The developers of this project accept the fact that traditional measures of student outcomes (for example, grades) are not useful or valid indicators for comparing the efficacy of courses with and without technology (Ehrmann and Zuniga, 1997). The reasons are well known: faculty are typically not trained assessors or test writers, they may grade *on the curve* and change tests and standards from semester to semester, and when they reengineer or transform their courses, they tend to change their tests and assessment methods, thus making comparisons with earlier classes impossible. The Flashlight Project notes that the transformation of courses through technology changes the nature of these courses, the pedagogical approaches used, and eventually the educational goals of the course. A class with technology and a class without it cannot be equivalent and any comparison between them that tries to assess the impact of technology will be invalid.

Instead, Flashlight Project developers use the findings of educational research as evidence and indirect indicators of increased learning. If certain educational conditions are met or increased as a result of technology—for example, active learning, faculty-student interaction, and rich and prompt feedback—then it is probable that learning outcomes have also improved and technology has indeed enhanced the learning environment. The Flashlight Current Student Inventory uses as its basis a set of acknowledged principles of learning, which are closely allied and overlap with the "seven principles of good practice in undergraduate education," developed by Chickering and Gamson (1987, 1991; for the technology applications of these principles, see Chickering and Ehrmann, 1996). The most important point about this approach is that it is not technology per se but the underlying pedagogy—the instructional design of the course—that makes the crucial difference in the learning environment. If this message alone were to come through in any of our reports and other communications, then we would consider our work to be a success.

Virginia Tech has embraced the Flashlight Project for another reason: as important as the work at Virginia Tech is, it is still an isolated venture. It is always more useful to enlarge one's efforts and be able to compare results to other courses, programs, and institutions. Doing so requires either a controlled experiment (which is both time consuming and logistically and politically difficult) or a standardized method or instrument that is used by many institutions, thus enabling comparisons to be made.

Doing Assessment: Getting Help

If Virginia Tech's case is in any way typical, many other institutions are also facing a crisis of assessment. New technologies, interventions, and programs are proliferating much faster than they can be assessed, given the paucity of available experts. Developers, already pressed for time and unskilled in evaluation, are nevertheless being asked to provide answers to difficult and problematic questions: for example, Do students learn more or more efficiently as a result of the developers' program or do any added benefits justify the costs? In order for institutions to make sense of these many and varied projects, they must be assessed—but how? One answer is to make use of available instruments, such as the Flashlight Project instrument described previously, and follow the recommendations described in other chapters in this volume. A concurrent approach is to use the expertise that already exists on one's own campus. In most cases this expertise resides in an office of institutional research (IR). IR personnel typically have a great deal of experience in working with the very entities with which technology developers are concerned: students, faculty, and departments. Similarly, they are experienced in the practical differences between assessment or evaluation and the kind of rigorous basic research in which social scientists engage. As described previously, assessment uses many of the methods of basic research but differs on practical and philosophical issues. However, for the relationship between IR staff and developers to prove beneficial, those involved must recognize several points.

First, the developer must realize that most IR offices are probably already working at or near full capacity. Typically, they must provide a constant stream of data for upper administration, the higher education supervisory board, and legislative committees. However, they are highly skilled in the theory and practice of designing and implementing quantitative studies within the settings of higher education. At a minimum they should be able to provide some consulting services to faculty developers who are embarking on a project.

Second, IR personnel must be approached early in the development process. A typical view of an assessment or evaluation is that it is a one-shot study performed when a project is nearly complete because it is thought that the effects or outcomes are the project's most important aspect. Unfortunately, by that time a great deal of valuable data has probably been lost, forever. Frequently, it is changes in conditions over time—trend analysis—that provide the most insight about the impact of an intervention. Therefore, the best time to consult with IR is during the planning stages, so that mechanisms can be installed and the right data can be captured when they are available and in a form that will be useful. In addition, the data must be captured consistently and at the proper intervals and then maintained in a healthy state. Furthermore, if conditions within the project change, knowledgeable decisions must be made about which new data to capture, and IR can provide help with making these decisions. IR can also provide help with planning for the delivery stage, that is, for analysis and reporting of the data that are gathered. Institutional researchers can help developers focus and clarify the ultimate purpose, use, and display of the data and the results of the study. Finally, at the strategic level, institutional researchers can give advice on the ultimate purpose and impact of the study as a whole—who might be interested in the results, the possible impact of the findings, and so forth. IR personnel typically have a great deal of experience in creating useful reports and making them available to the appropriate audience.

However, developers should not expect IR offices to help with all the types of studies described here. Typically, most IR personnel have strong quantitative backgrounds. Although they can offer their perspective on its usefulness, qualitative research may be out of their area of expertise. For example, Virginia's State Council of Higher Education decided only in 1998 to accept some limited qualitative data (student satisfaction responses) from state institutions as part of their periodic reports. In addition, faculty developers should not expect IR personnel to be experts in new technologies or new teaching approaches. A process of education must take place, but with good communication they can usually learn enough, and quickly enough, to help design a useful assessment. Therefore, the important points to be communicated from faculty developers to institutional researchers are not merely the technology and its application but the nature of the pedagogical transformation itself. Most people in or out of higher education implicitly assume that the old models still apply and that knowledge is *delivered* to the student by lecture and test. It is more likely, however, that new teaching and learning models, new modes of discourse, and asynchronous interaction will form the basis of course or program transformations, and these new models must be the starting point for an assessment design.

References

Chickering, A., and Ehrmann, S. C. "Implementing the Seven Principles: Technology as Lever." *AAHE Bulletin,* Oct. 1996, pp. 3–6. [www.aahe.org/technology/ehrmann.htm].

Chickering, A., and Gamson, Z. "Seven Principles of Good Practice in Undergraduate Education." *AAHE Bulletin,* 1987, *39* (7), 3–7.

Chickering, A., and Gamson, Z. (eds.). *Applying the Seven Principles for Good Practice in Undergraduate Education.* New Directions for Teaching and Learning, no. 47. San Francisco: Jossey-Bass, 1991.

Denzin, N. K., and Lincoln, Y. S. (eds.). *Handbook of Qualitative Research.* Thousand Oaks, Calif.: Sage, 1994.

Ehrmann, S. C., and Zuniga, R. E. *The Flashlight Evaluation Handbook.* Washington, D.C.: American Association for Higher Education, 1997.

Gregorian, V., Hawkins, B. L., and Taylor, M. "Integrating Information Technologies: A Research University Perspective." *CAUSE/EFFECT,* Winter 1992, pp. 2–12.

McClure, C. R., and Lopata, C. L. *Assessing the Academic Networked Environment: Strategies and Options.* Washington, D.C.: Coalition for Networked Information, 1996: [www.cni.org/projects/assessing].

Miles, M. B., and Huberman, A. M. *Qualitative Data Analysis: An Expanded Sourcebook.* (2nd ed.) Thousand Oaks, Calif.: Sage, 1994.

Patton, M. Q. *Qualitative Evaluation and Research Methods.* (2nd ed.) Thousand Oaks, Calif.: Sage, 1990.

Ray, N. M., and Minch, R. P. "Computer Anxiety and Alienation: Toward a Definitive and Parsimonious Measure." *Human Factors,* 1990, *32* (4), 477–491.

State Council of Higher Education for Virginia. Presentation on Preliminary Restructuring Progress. [www.schev.edu/wumedia/cn95.html]. June 1995.

Sykes, C. J. *The Hollow Men: Politics and Corruption in Higher Education.* Washington, D.C.: Regnery, 1990.

Taylor, C. D., Roy, L., and Moore, J. F. *ACCESS: Asynchronous Communication Courses to Enable Student Success.* A report submitted to the Alfred P. Sloan Foundation by Educational Technologies/Instructional Services, Virginia Polytechnic Institute and State University, July 1997. [www.edtech.vt.edu/access].

Twigg, C. "The Need for a National Learning Infrastructure." *Educom Review,* Sept.–Oct. 1994, pp. 16–20. [www.educause.edu/pub/er/review/reviewarticles/29516.html].

University Task Force on the Impact of Digital Technology on the Classroom Environment. *Report of the University Task Force on the Impact of Digital Technology on the Classroom Environment.* Roanoke: Virginia Polytechnic Institute and State University, 1989.

Virginia Commission on the University of the Twenty-First Century. *The Case for Change.* Richmond: Commonwealth of Virginia, 1990.

Virginia Polytechnic Institute and State University. *Phase II: Instructional Development Initiative.* Blacksburg: Virginia Polytechnic Institute and State University, May 1995.

Walzer, P. "Professors Not Often in Class." *Roanoke Times and World News,* Sept. 12–14, 1993, p. 1.

C. DAVID TAYLOR *is director of educational assessment and technology at the University of Texas Health Science Center at Houston, Dental Branch, and adjunct associate professor in the Department of Dental Public Health and Dental Hygiene. Previously he was assessment project manager for instructional innovations at Virginia Polytechnic Institute and State University.*

JOANNE D. EUSTIS *is director of the university library at Case Western Reserve University. She formerly held a variety of positions spanning sixteen years at Virginia Polytechnic Institute and State University.*

This chapter discusses issues and practices in information management, with a primary focus on the importance of information management to the institutional research and assessment community.

Institution-Wide Information Management and Its Assessment

Gerald Bernbom

The information revolution, in which higher education has played so significant a role, has in large measure been characterized by the popular media as the story of an *information technology* revolution: how the speed of computation continues to increase through advances in high-performance computing, how the speed of communication increases through advances in high-performance networks, how the size of microchips is shrinking, how access to worldwide data networks is becoming ubiquitous, how wireless communications technology is exploding, how electronic commerce is growing, and so much more.

Of equal if not greater significance, however, is the information revolution as a story about *information itself*: how information is created and kept safe, how it is used and who uses it, what it costs to collect and save it, what its value is, and how that value is affected by its timeliness, accuracy, and accessibility.

This chapter discusses issues and practices in information management, as it is carried out by a variety of professionals in the information and information technology fields, with a primary focus on the importance of information management to the institutional research and assessment community.

A program of institutional assessment may focus its attention directly on information management, assessing how well information is being managed, at what cost, to what uses it is being put, and to what effect. A thorough evaluation of an institution's information technology investments will also assess practices in the more specific fields of data administration, records management, and information resource management. This chapter provides institutional researchers with an overview and perspective on information management practices, so that these practices can be assessed either specifically or as part of an overall assessment of information technology.

In addition, good information management helps ensure that the data needed to conduct institutional assessment and planning are available when they are needed and in the form they are needed. Thus this chapter also provides institutional researchers with an overview of information management so that they may influence management practices and make them more likely to provide information that is useful in the conduct of institutional assessment and planning.

Scope of Information Management

Information has intrinsic value to an institution. As McGee and Prusak (1993) state, "Information technology investments create no more advantage or productivity, by themselves, than do investments in new machine tools. . . . The value of information technology depends on information and the role of information in organizations" (pp. 2–3).

At the same time, computing and communication technologies can change the value of information. Information technology may add value by making information more available or useful to an institution or by creating new information to meet an operational or decision-making need. Information technology may also subtract value by making information more vulnerable to theft, destruction, or misuse, thus increasing the institution's liability.

Assessment measures related to information and information technology may focus on this key question: How do information technology and information management practices add to, or subtract from, the value of information to our institution? Or, put another way, What potential value is being lost due to shortcomings in our institution's information management practices?

In considering information management it is essential to define what kinds of information we are talking about. Most definitely, the focus includes what might be called administrative data, enterprise data, management information, or institutional records. These data include information about employees and students, purchases and payments, equipment inventories, student transcripts, and class rosters. Such data, comprising enterprise databases and institutional records, will be the primary topic of this chapter.

Typically excluded from consideration in data administration or information resource management (and thus also from this chapter) is much of what is referred to as the *scholarly record*. Examples of such materials include research results, literary and creative works, and experimental data; these are in the domain of scholars, libraries, and information science.

This division of territory leaves behind a rich, messy middle ground of semiorganized, computerized information created and maintained in some fashion by a college or university and its members. In this category might be computerized instructional materials; records of electronic communication among scholars and students; various factual databases, compilations, or other networked information resources; and so forth. In the 1980s, some computerized information of this sort was stored on a relatively small number of time-share computers, including those that hosted campuswide information systems (CWISs), or was scattered among a number of distributed (and largely disconnected) desktop computers. With the tremendous growth of the World Wide Web and the more recent rise of the campus intranet (a successor to the CWIS), there is a growing body of information that could be organized and actively managed and also assessed for its potential value to the institution. By and large these steps are being taken neither by librarians nor by data administrators or records managers. This body of *informal institutional data* is not a primary focus of this chapter but will be revisited at the end as a topic worthy of future evaluation.

The following sections of this chapter outline some basic concepts of information management and suggest assessment issues related to each. The concept of *information architecture* deals with the various uses to which an institution puts information and the implications this has for the organization and management of institutional data. *Information policy* constitutes the rules and guidelines an institution develops to structure its information management activities. *Data administration* is the set of practices and priorities that seek to preserve and enhance the value of information. And the concept of an *institution-wide view of information* suggests ways to avoid splintering and fragmentation of data within an institution.

Information Architecture: Multiple Uses of Information

Fundamental to the practice of information management is the understanding that information serves multiple purposes in an institution and that it should be organized and managed in different ways depending on its use. For example, a lab assistant who wants to reorder a specific item may need information from an earlier individual purchase requisition. A detailed list of past purchases—item, vendor, and price—may be needed by a lab manager who is considering whether to establish a volume purchase agreement with certain vendors. A summary of the total amount spent on lab equipment, computer equipment, and other capital equipment might be needed by a department head who needs to assess her current budget position and decide whether to make some specific purchase. An archivist or historian who is studying the institutional history of technology infusion might want to know when purchases of personal computers first exceeded purchases of typewriters or when laser printers were first purchased by departments and individual faculty.

Although these cases all deal with information about purchases, the different users need different amounts of information at different levels of detail and with different specific details, depending on what the user is doing.

A key purpose of an information architecture is to describe how information is organized, how it is used, and how information gathered or used for one purpose is transformed to be used for another purpose. Assessing the value of information, and how well it is being managed, requires understanding how the information is being used or is meant to be used. Five essential uses of information in an organization are processing transactions, supporting decision making, assessing performance, archiving institutional history, and providing evidence of institutional actions.

Transactions. Institutional information is frequently used in the conduct of routine business or administrative transactions: registering a student in a course, for example, or paying an employee or disbursing a financial aid award. Information adds value to these transactions by enabling the associated work activity or making it more effective. Information used in transaction processing is valued for its timeliness and accuracy, and typically such information must be represented with a high level of detail and specificity. Often transaction processing is the original source of the data in an information system.

Decisions. Information is frequently used for analysis and decision making in an institution. This information is typically fairly stable, consisting of extracts, or snapshots, of data taken from transaction processing systems for use in decision support. Such *frozen* information is often derived from multiple sources, which might be internal to the college or university (for example, student enrollment data, budget data, faculty teaching data) or external (for example, age and income demographics). Added value comes when information is organized so that data from one source can be compared to, combined with, or related to data from other sources.

Assessment. Institutional data are essential to the conduct of institutional research and assessment. Information used for assessment is typically very stable. For example, it might include *census* data, in which data values are recorded at institutionally agreed-upon dates or time points (for example, the first day of classes). This information is often longitudinal, to reveal change over time or to show the effect of some intervention. As well, information used in assessment should be related to significant performance measures of interest to the institution.

A number of information architecture frameworks identify the use of information for transactions, decisions, and, to some extent, assessment (see, for example, Inmon, 1989, or Apple Computer Corporation, 1992). Less commonly addressed is the use of information for preserving institutional history or managing institutional liability. Helen Samuels (1992) provides a very useful orientation to the archival use of information based on the analysis of institutional functions. And David Bearman (1994) provides an analysis of the requirements for using electronic information as evidence.

Archives. The archives of a college or university record and preserve information about the institution. Archival information allows a history of the institution to be assembled through a documentary record of institutional activity. To be of archival value, information must be evaluated and selected as relevant to the institution's mission or purpose, preserved for the long-term, and organized and described so that it may be searched and retrieved. Essential to the evaluation and selection of archival information is a functional analysis of the institution, to identify the key activities that should be documented (see Samuels, 1992). It is also important that historical records be kept static and unchanged. That is, no one should be permitted to change the history of the institution by manipulating archives.

Evidence. Information serves the institution when it provides the evidence of institutional actions that is necessary to comply with laws or regulations. Information for evidence should be accurate and consistent, and only authorized individuals should have permission to create or modify it. A series of *functional requirements* for the evidential value of electronic records has been developed as part of a research program funded by the National Historic Publications and Records Commission (see for example Cox, 1994; Barry, 1996; Bantin and Bernbom, 1996).

Information Policy

An information policy provides a set of rules for the information behavior of an institution and its members. In some cases rules may precisely describe some behavior that is required (for example, that you must change your password every thirty days) or is prohibited (for example, that you may not disclose confidential information to a third party). In other cases a rule may describe a process or procedure by which an issue is addressed or a dispute is settled. The grounds for this set of rules may be established through a policy framework that states assumptions, establishes principles, and describes institutional values (see for example Graves, Jenkins, and Parker, 1995). This framework may be accompanied by an organizational mechanism—an office, officer, or committee—charged to interpret the principles and guidelines outlined in the policy.

The importance of an information policy framework cannot be overstated. The policy framework provides the rules of engagement by which more specific rules or policies are developed. It affords the institution an opportunity to describe how it wishes to use and manage information of all types, paper records as well as electronic databases, and how it wants to assign the responsibility and authority associated with managing and using institutional information. An information policy framework is thus much more than a policy on computer use or a policy on information technology. Rather, as was emphasized earlier, it deals with *information itself*, in its various forms and uses.

Once the information policy framework is established, specific rules are needed as issues arise in each phase of the information life cycle: creation, storage, maintenance, use and access, and preservation or disposal.

Creation. A typical issue in the creation of information arises when information created or captured by one department is needed by others. Because of the cost or effort involved, the department that captures the data may consider only its own requirements, not those of others. Information policy is needed to ensure that information is available institution-wide without duplication but also at a reasonable expense to the individual department on whom the burden of creation is placed.

Storage. Information standards are needed so that data are stored in such a way that they can be shared (and understood) across the institution and so that data from different sources can be combined, compared, related, and so forth. The way in which information is stored is often a direct outcome of the way in which it is captured. Information policy can provide the structure for setting standards for information storage and for resolving differences.

Maintenance. Some typical maintenance issues involve assigning responsibility for keeping data current and for organizing and managing data in ways appropriate to various uses. As with information capture, the key issue often involves resources: who will invest the effort to maintain the data and who will benefit from that effort.

Use and Access. A wide range of issues arises with respect to information use, among them rules about access to data and personal privacy. For student records and some other types of institutional data, concerns for privacy may also involve legal restrictions or requirements. Other issues of information access involve institutional accountability or, for public institutions, information disclosure requirements established by *open records* laws.

Preservation or Disposal. Among the issues that information policy can address are the establishment of minimal requirements for preserving electronic records as evidence of business or administrative actions and the setting of guidelines for preserving electronic records in order to document an institution's history.

In all the cases typified by the preceding examples the intent of information policy is to influence the information behavior of individuals and the organizations they represent within an institution. One important thrust of this influence is to promote certain norms of behavior and to discourage extremes, especially to discourage or prohibit behavior that is illegal or harmful.

Establishing norms of behavior in an institution often requires finding a balance among multiple conflicting values. Accountability may favor broad and relatively unrestricted access to information, whereas concerns for privacy may favor restrictions. Academic freedom may favor few limits on what may be said, spoken, sent by e-mail, or published on the Web; community ethical values or the value of collegiality may favor more restraints on discourse.

Davenport, Eccles, and Prusak (1992), in a pioneering essay, observed that information management and the shaping of an organization's information behavior is in large measure a political process. The establishment of information policy in particular—establishing institutional rules of conduct and defining processes for settling disputes—calls for political analysis and judgment.

Success depends on a long-term commitment to clear understanding and to reaching some level of agreement about institutional values. This is a two-part process. Areas of agreement are documented as foundations of information policy, and areas of disagreement are kept open for discussion. This approach to information politics is termed *federalism* and is based on consensus and negotiation. It avoids peremptory conclusions and keeps all parties engaged, thus avoiding the pitfalls that Davenport and his colleagues refer to as *feudalism, monarchy,* and *anarchy*—political states in which information management is fragmented among warring parties or seized, at least temporarily, by a central authority or in which there is no order or agreement at all about information and its uses.

Implementing information policy, especially in a political environment, depends on a combination of education and advocacy. Education ensures that rules of information behavior that have been agreed to are widely known and well understood and likewise that processes for voicing disagreements or settling disputes about information are advertised and used when needed. An educational program in information management also seeks to advance progress on issues of information policy that are still under discussion; for instance, it might use case studies and scenarios to clarify the issues and the values that might be at stake in settling them. Advocacy promotes institution-wide values for information management, seeking the common good or the greater institutional good and helping the institution steer away from information policy choices that lead to fragmentation or conflict.

Data Administration: Information Management Processes

In many enterprises, including many colleges and universities, the implementation of information policy and the overall guidance of information management practices are the responsibility of a data administration unit or function. The present chapter does not make a significant distinction between *data* and *information.* The line between them has never been terribly clear and often depends on the perspective of the viewer. (One person's data is another's information.) But the term *data administration* is in wide use to refer to a field of professional practice that is aligned with other information and information technology disciplines. As I once described it in an introductory article on the subject (Bernbom, 1991), "data administration is the application of formal rules and methods to the management of an organization's data resources. As an entity in an organization, data administration may take on various forms: as a line function within the IS organization, as a staff function reporting to a senior administrator in such areas as Information Technology or Administration and Finance, or as a 'virtual' function where responsibilities of data administration are shared among several areas of the organization" (p. 12). Regardless of the data administration function's organizational form, an important part of that function is to promote rules, methods, and practices that enhance the quality of institutional information.

Also worth noting is that data administration is almost always affiliated in some way with the information technology activities and organization of an institution, and so its attention is typically focused on computerized databases of centrally managed information. Information management is conceived of more broadly and deals not only with computerized data but with information in all forms (including paper records) and from all sources. Nevertheless, the principal concern of data administration, ensuring information quality, can be applied equally well to information from many sources and in any form.

Six specific imperatives in data administration for ensuring information quality can be stated:

Information should be authentic. The information that an institution collects and maintains should be a faithful model of the real world. It should be organized and represented in a way that faithfully conveys the relevant facts. Interpretation of the information should be unambiguous.

Information should be authoritative. An authoritative source of information should exist that may be consulted to determine any fact of significance to the institution. If information is replicated, its multiple instances should be consistent with the authoritative source.

Information should be accurate. Facts should be represented truthfully. When facts change, the information that represents them should change too.

Information should be shared. Information increases in value when it is put to use. Information loses value when it is misused or when opportunities for its productive use are lost.

Information should be intelligible. Users need contextual information about the institutional information they are using. Data definitions, descriptions, and documentation help make institutional information intelligible to users.

Information should be secure. All information should be protected from unauthorized or accidental corruption or destruction. As well, some information should be protected from inappropriate disclosure or improper use.

In data administration substantial energy and attention is given especially to information security. This emphasis is spurred on by the increasing level of risk that results from increased reliance on electronic information and communications, owing to the increasing sophistication of hackers and crackers who might threaten the security and integrity of an institution's information resources and to the ease with which a single individual (for example, a disgruntled employee) can destroy large masses of data and even backup copies with only a few keystrokes in only a few minutes.

There is, to begin, the risk of damage to institutional information. This may be either accidental or intentional and may result in the unauthorized destruction or alteration of information. Specific risks include computer viruses, computer break-ins, and stolen or misappropriated passwords, which can and often do result in the loss of information. This risk is amplified if users within the institution do not recognize the dangers or do not make use of available protections (for example, virus-scanning software or rules for choosing passwords).

A second area of risk that information management practices must address is the risk of inappropriate disclosure of information. This too may be either accidental or intentional and may result in a variety of harms: loss of individual privacy, loss of competitive advantage, exposure of sensitive information, or damage to reputation. The risks from within the institution may arise when users do not know the rules or constraints on the use of information or when the institution does not have such rules.

Technologies to address issues of security include encryption, which stores and transmits information encoded so that only sender and receiver can read it; authentication, which requires individuals to offer credentials to prove their identity to a computer system or network; and authorization, which establishes permissions for who may do what and enforces them through system restrictions.

Institution-Wide View of Information

A successful data administration program and an effective set of information management practices will lead to a view of information as an institution-wide resource, a view of information that is integrated and not fragmented.

At some institutions the same information may be collected multiple times or may be stored and maintained in two or more separate places. In some cases what appears to be the same item of information in two separate locations has a different meaning in each place. This fragmentation of information and its meaning may be the result of organizational structure (as when two departments separately collect student address information or have different definitions of what a *local address* is). Or the fragmentation may be an artifact of information systems design (as when the payroll system and the accounting system each maintain their own tables of valid university accounts or have their own definitions of what an *account* is).

One goal of information management practice is to limit or eliminate redundancy, seeking to influence organizations and the design of their information systems so that information is captured once, stored in a single authoritative location, and replicated as needed throughout the institution.

A second goal is to establish common definitions and values for information, used across the institution. For various departments and individuals to share the same information, they have to agree to use that information in the same way and to apply the same meaning to it.

A third goal is to help develop agreements about responsibility for creating or maintaining information, about exchanging information, and about permission to access information. These agreements will develop over time, and ongoing attention is needed to ensure their continued success.

A fourth goal is to promote the view of institutional information as a shared resource, not something that is *owned* by individuals or departments.

A final goal for information management is the integration and reintegration of information, both from the institution's perspective (yielding increased effectiveness and improved communication across organizational boundaries) and from the individual user's perspective (providing an information environment that is useful and usable).

In promoting information management goals, the data administration function on a college or university campus may find allies among others having an institution-wide view of information. These others are likely to include archivists, who are concerned with the documentary record of the entire institution; auditors, who are typically concerned with the integrity and accuracy of information processes throughout the institution; information security officers, who seek to protect the integrity of information without undue overhead or restraints on use; and institutional researchers, who need an information environment that combines and collects data from multiple sources into a single, usable resource. A successful partnership in institution-wide information management might be crafted from the resources of these five potential allies in the information professions.

The ideas and issues I have been discussing suggest a number of areas in which institutional researchers can assess an institution's information management practices, perhaps as part of an overall evaluation of information technology. Exhibit 5.1 presents an assessment checklist.

Informal Information Environments

As I mentioned previously, in addition to formal enterprise information, a vast amount of semiorganized, computerized information is created and maintained on virtually every college and university campus. First known as campuswide information systems (CWISs), now referred to as intranets, these loose collections largely fall outside the scope of formal information management practices. Nevertheless the value and utility of these networked information environments depend upon such practices: "The key issue for CWIS management is the management of content: selecting what to include, organizing it, giving each item or selection a meaningful name, keeping the content up to date, and presenting the information in a usable fashion" (Bernbom, 1993, p. 3).

The evaluation checklist for institutional information (Exhibit 5.1) suggests a starting point for assessing the management of an institution's informal information environment as well. As a first approximation, the following groups of questions could be addressed:

- Is there an information architecture for the campus intranet? Does the information on the campus intranet fit into a documented information architecture?
- Are there information policies and a policy framework that govern the creation, maintenance, use, and preservation of information on the campus intranet?
- Is there an institutional function responsible for managing information on the campus intranet? Does the institution have formal practices in place to ensure the accuracy, security, and accessibility of intranet information?
- Do institutional arrangements for dealing with information as an institution-wide resource apply to information on the campus intranet? For example, are there standards or procedures for reducing redundancy or negotiating access rights to information?

Exhibit 5.1. Assessing Information Management Practices: A Checklist

1. Describe the scope of the institution's information management practices. What kinds of information are included? What kinds are not?
2. Does the institution have an information architecture? Is it documented? Is it implemented?
3. Does the information architecture address the use of information for
   a. Transaction processing?
   b. Decision making?
   c. Assessment and institutional research?
   d. Archiving and institutional history?
   e. Evidence of institutional activity?
4. Does the institution have an information policy framework? Is it effectively implemented? Has it produced specific, written information policies?
5. Do the information policies of the institution address
   a. The creation or capture of information?
   b. The storage of information?
   c. The maintenance of information?
   d. The use of and access to information?
   e. The preservation and disposal of information?
6. Is there a program of education and advocacy to support the implementation and ongoing development of the institution's information policy?
7. Does the institution have a data administration function?
8. Is the data administration function responsible for
   a. Information quality?
   b. Information sharing?
   c. Information security?
9. Is there an institution-wide view of information?
10. Are there standards or procedures
    a. To reduce or eliminate data redundancy?
    b. To find common definitions for information items?
11. Is there a mechanism to establish or negotiate agreements about information access?
12. Is there a mechanism to establish or negotiate agreements about creating and maintaining information?

The boundary between institutional information environments that are formally managed and these informal information environments is becoming increasingly blurred. Both overall assessments of information technology or more focused evaluations of information management practices will necessarily include some consideration of intranets and campuswide information systems.

Assessment Data and Institutional Measures

Finally, most institutions also possess a body of *local assessment data*—survey results, classroom and departmental assessment instruments, cost and quality measures, or other performance measures. The institutional research function of an institution may also gather national or regional demographic data, trend indicators, or other measures related to significant institutional activities or measures of performance.

All too often these important information resources fall outside the scope of an institution's information policy, information architecture, established data administration practices, and institution-wide information strategies. Yet these assessment and institutional research data are valuable information resources that need active and careful management.

Again, the checklist in Exhibit 5.1 can provide a starting place for evaluating how well institutional research and assessment data are being managed. For example: Do the institution's information policies address the use of data gathered for assessment: is it clear who may use these assessment data and for what purposes? Do different assessment activities define and use information in the same way: do measures of institutional performance have a single meaning?

Institutional researchers play a key role in the collection, management, and use of information for institutional assessment and decision making. They are also in a position to take a truly institution-wide view of information and to see the interconnections among data having different origins within the institution. Yet their own data, whether from local assessment instruments and performance measures or from national and regional demographic sources, are as much in need of information management as any other information resource of the institution.

The ideas and guidelines suggested in this chapter may help institutional researchers assess information management on an institution-wide basis, either in an individual assessment or during an overall assessment of the institution's information technology, and also apply these principles to their own information management activities.

References

Apple Computer Corporation. *Introduction to VITAL: Designing Information Systems for the 1990s.* Cupertino, Calif.: Apple Computer Corp., 1992.

Bantin, P., and Bernbom, G. "The Indiana University Electronic Records Project: Analyzing Functions, Identifying Transactions, and Evaluating Recordkeeping Systems: A Report on Methodology." *Archives and Museum Informatics,* 1996, *10* (3), 246–266.

Barry, R. E. "Summary of a Study of the World Bank's Electronic Filing System Using the University of Pittsburgh Project Functional Requirements for Recordkeeping as an Assessment Tool." [www.lis.pitt.edu/~nhprc/reb-wb.html]. Feb. 1, 1996.

Bearman, D. *Electronic Evidence: Strategies for Managing Records in Contemporary Organizations.* Pittsburgh, Pa.: Archives and Museum Informatics, 1994.

Bernbom, G. "Data Administration and Distributed Data Processing." *CAUSE/EFFECT,* 1991, *14* (4), 8–15. [www.educause.edu/ir/library/text/cem9142.txt].

Bernbom, G. "Campus-Wide Information Systems: Managing Information Content." *CAUSE/EFFECT,* 1993, *16* (4), 3–5. [www.educause.edu/ir/library/text/cem9341.txt].

Cox, R. J. "Re-Discovering the Archival Mission: The Recordkeeping Functional Requirements Project at the University of Pittsburgh: A Progress Report." *Archives and Museum Informatics,* 1994, *8* (4), 279–300.

Davenport, T. H., Eccles, R. G., and Prusak, L. "Information Politics." *Sloan Management Review,* 1992, *34* (1), 53–65.

Graves, B., Jenkins, C., and Parker, A. "Development of an Electronic Information Policy Framework." *CAUSE/EFFECT,* 1995, *18* (2), 15–23. [www.educause.edu/ir/library/text/cem9524.txt].

Inmon, W. H. *Data Architecture: The Information Paradigm.* Wellesley, Mass.: QED, 1989.

McGee, J., and Prusak, L. *Managing Information Strategically.* New York: Wiley, 1993.

Samuels, H. W. *Varsity Letters: Documenting Modern Colleges and Universities.* Metuchen, N.J.: Society of American Archivists and Scarecrow Press, 1992.

GERALD BERNBOM is special assistant for digital libraries and distance education in the Office of the Vice President for Information Technology at Indiana University.

INDEX

ABC. *See* Activity-based costing

ABM. *See* Activity-based management

ACCESS project. *See* Asynchronous Communications Courses to Ensure Student Success (ACCESS)

Ackerman, E., 28

Action Request software (Remedy Corporation), 30

Activity-based costing (ABC), 40–42, 45, 50

Activity-based management (ABM), 40

Adams, K. H., 5, 37

Adobe Illustrator, 44

Alfred P. Sloan Foundation, 29, 61

Allmayer, D., 5, 37

American Association for Higher Education, Teaching, Learning, and Technology Affiliate (TLT Group), 25

Antolovic, L. G., 5, 37

Apple Computer Corporation, 50, 74

Applications, top ten, for NT and Macintosh computers in IU Bloomington campus STCs, 44

ARL. *See* Association of Research Libraries

ARL Newsletter, 25

Assessing the Academic Networked Environment: Strategies and Options (McClure and Lopata), 24, 26, 65

Assessment: of academic networked environment, 21–34; and Coalition for Network Information (CNI) assessment project, 26–31; methodologies for, 65–68; and overview of assessment efforts, 23–26

Assessment data, 82

Association of Research Libraries (ARL), 21, 24, 25, 34

Astin, A. W., 52

Asynchronous Communications Courses to Ensure Student Success (ACCESS), 29, 58, 60–62, 66

Asynchronous learning, 57, 61

Asynchronous transfer mode (ATM), 62

Augmentation, 51–52

Automation, 51–52

Ayersman, D. J., 28

Balanced scorecard, 39, 48–50

Baliles, G., 56

Banta, T. W., 52

Bantin, P., 75

Barry, R. E., 75

Bate, P., 39

Bates, A. W., 26

Bearman, D., 74

Bell Atlantic, 60

Bernbom, G., 6, 21, 71, 75, 77, 80

Black, K. E., 52

Blacksburg Electronic Village (BEV), 60

Blixrud, J. C., 25

Brown University, 27–29, 55

California State University (CSU), 25

Calvert, T., 26

Campbell, G., 28

Campus Computing Survey (Green), 24

Campus networks: background to, 22–23; five elements in, 23–24; guidelines for assessing impact of, 34

Campuswide information systems (CWISs), 73, 80

Canada, 26

Carnegie credit, 2

Carroll, L., 37

CAUSE, 21, 24

CAUSE survey, 1

Chemical Abstracts database, 30

Chickering, A., 68

Chief information officer (CIO), role of, 12

Chodorow, S., 2

Client-server architecture, versus mainframe infrastructure, 60

CNI. *See* Coalition for Networked Information

Coalition for Networked Information (CNI), 4, 21, 22, 26–27, 32–34, 63–64

Coalition for Networked Information (CNI) Assessing the Academic Networked Environment project: background to, 21–22; and Brown University, 28–29; and Dartmouth College Computing Services, 29–30; and facilitation of teaching and learning, 27–29; fundamental conundrum in, 4; and Gettysburg College, 31; and help desks, 29–30; and King's College, London, 31; lessons learned from, 32–33; and library and

Back Issue/Subscription Order Form

Copy or detach and send to:
Jossey-Bass Inc., Publishers, 350 Sansome Street, San Francisco CA 94104-1342

Call or fax toll free!
Phone 888-378-2537 6AM-5PM PST; Fax 800-605-2665

Back issues   Please send me the following issues at $23 each:
(Important: please include series initials and issue number, such as IR90)

1. IR _____

_____

_____

$ _____ Total for single issues

$ _____ Shipping charges (for single issues *only;* subscriptions are exempt from shipping charges): Up to $30, add $5^{50} • $30^{01}–$50, add $6^{50} $50^{01}–$75, add $7^{50} • $75^{01}–$100, add $9 • $100^{01}–$150, add $10 Over $150, call for shipping charge

Subscriptions   Please ❑ start   ❑ renew my subscription to *New Directions for Institutional Research* for the year 1999 at the following rate:

❑ Individual $56   ❑ Institutional $95
NOTE: Subscriptions are quarterly, and are for the calendar year only. Subscriptions begin with the spring issue of the year indicated above. For shipping outside the U.S., please add $25.

$ _____ Total single issues and subscriptions (CA, IN, NJ, NY and DC residents, add sales tax for single issues. NY and DC residents must include shipping charges when calculating sales tax. NY and Canadian residents only, add sales tax for subscriptions.)

❑ Payment enclosed (U.S. check or money order only)

❑ VISA, MC, AmEx, Discover Card #_____ Exp. date_____

Signature _____ Day phone _____

❑ Bill me (U.S. institutional orders only. Purchase order required.)

Purchase order #_____

Name _____

Address _____

_____

_____

Phone_____ E-mail _____

For more information about Jossey-Bass Publishers, visit our Web site at:
www.josseybass.com   **PRIORITY CODE = ND1**